FROM INTENT TO IMPACT

Happy re   ,
Look forward to
seeing you on
        Monday :)
    Love
Vanessa and
    Team MA!

FROM INTENT TO IMPACT: THE NEW BLUEPRINT FOR INCLUSION

BY

ASIF SADIQ MBE

United Kingdom – North America – Japan
India – Malaysia – China

Emerald Publishing Limited
Emerald Publishing, Floor 5, Northspring, 21-23 Wellington Street, Leeds LS1 4DL.

First edition 2025

Copyright © 2025 Asif Sadiq.
Published under exclusive licence by Emerald Publishing Limited.

Reprints and permissions service
Contact: www.copyright.com

No part of this book may be reproduced, stored in a retrieval system, transmitted in any form or by any means electronic, mechanical, photocopying, recording or otherwise without either the prior written permission of the publisher or a licence permitting restricted copying issued in the UK by The Copyright Licensing Agency and in the USA by The Copyright Clearance Center. No responsibility is accepted for the accuracy of information contained in the text, illustrations or advertisements. The opinions expressed in these chapters are not necessarily those of the Author or the publisher.

British Library Cataloguing in Publication Data
A catalogue record for this book is available from the British Library

ISBN: 978-1-80455-020-5 (Print)
ISBN: 978-1-80455-017-5 (Online)
ISBN: 978-1-80455-019-9 (Epub)

Printed and bound by CPI Group (UK) Ltd, Croydon, CR0 4YY

INVESTOR IN PEOPLE

CONTENTS

Foreword   vii

1. The Journey from Diversity and Inclusion to Belonging   1
2. What to Focus on in An Ever-Evolving Space   17
3. Deepening Your Understanding of Inclusion   29
4. Inclusion Strategies for Workplace Revolution   41
5. Developing Strategies That Impact Profitability and Customer Engagement   53
6. Creating Meaningful Inclusion Programmes and Initiatives   75
7. Measuring and Tracking Inclusion Impact and Progress   89
8. Embedding Inclusion into Every Stage of the Employee Lifecycle   101
9. Navigating Challenges: Addressing Resistance and Barriers   115

FOREWORD

When I first began my journey in the inclusion space, the conversation looked very different. At the time, diversity was often limited to checklists, and inclusion was something spoken about – but rarely felt. Over the years, I've had the privilege of witnessing this space evolve, deepen, and mature. But I've also seen the challenges, the resistance, and the critical need to shift from surface-level initiatives to building cultures where people genuinely belong.

This book is the product of years of learning – not only through professional experiences but through listening. Listening to employees who felt unseen. To leaders who wanted to do better but weren't sure how. To teams who knew that culture is not built in the boardroom, but in every interaction, every policy, every unspoken norm.

I've written this book for those who believe that inclusion is more than a programme – it's a mindset, a responsibility, and an opportunity. It's for those who understand that culture doesn't change overnight, but also that every action counts. And it's especially for those who are ready to move beyond theory and start building inclusion into the very DNA of their organizations.

In these pages, I share what I've learned about embedding inclusion meaningfully – across systems, strategies, and structures – in ways that drive real impact. Whether you're just beginning your inclusion journey or are deep in the work, I hope this book challenges you, supports you, and reminds you that inclusion is not a destination – it's a continuous journey we walk together.

Thank you for being part of this work.

Asif Sadiq, MBE

In a world where diversity and inclusion are more than just buzzwords but essential principles for thriving organizations, the need for thoughtful, actionable, and transformative guidance has never been greater. This is precisely what Asif Sadiq delivers in his latest work. As a pioneering thought leader in the inclusion space, Asif blends years of experience with a deep understanding of the cultural, social, and organizational nuances that shape the workplace and society today.

What makes this book particularly compelling is Asif's ability to balance the theoretical with the practical. He acknowledges that inclusion work is not simply about implementing policies or checking boxes – it is about creating a seismic cultural shift that transforms how we think, act, and lead. This transformation requires a willingness to challenge the status quo, confront uncomfortable truths, and commit to a journey of continuous learning and growth. Asif leads readers through this process with clarity and compassion, offering tools and strategies that are as actionable as they are visionary.

Christopher Rainey
Host HR Leaders Podcast/ Co-founder, HR Leaders/Atlas Copilot

At the heart of Asif's message is the belief that inclusion is not an isolated initiative but a cornerstone of organizational success. Drawing from his extensive global experience, Asif underscores the critical importance of embedding inclusion into the fabric of an organization – integrating it into leadership, decision-making, and day-to-day operations. This holistic approach is what sets his work apart. He doesn't just tell organizations *what* to do; he shows them *how* to do it in a way that is sustainable, authentic, and impactful.

This book is more than a guide; it is a call to action for leaders, practitioners, and anyone committed to creating equitable and inclusive spaces. Asif doesn't shy away from the complexities of inclusion work. Instead, he invites readers to embrace these challenges as opportunities for growth and innovation. He highlights the importance of adaptability, recognizing that inclusion efforts must evolve alongside the changing dynamics of our workplaces and communities.

Okorie Ramsey, CPA, CGMA, PMP
Past AICPA and Association Global Board & Committee Chair

This book is not only for leaders or Diversity professionals – it is for anyone who wants to make a difference. Asif's writing reminds us that the journey towards equity and inclusion is a shared responsibility. Whether you are a CEO shaping company culture, an employee advocating for change, or an individual seeking to broaden your understanding, this book offers valuable insights that resonate across levels and industries.

As you embark on this journey with Asif as your guide, prepare to be inspired, challenged, and empowered. This work is not just a roadmap for navigating inclusion in the modern world – it is a manifesto for creating a future where diversity is celebrated, equity is prioritized, and inclusion is the norm. Let this book serve as your companion and catalyst as you contribute to building the equitable and inclusive world we all aspire to achieve.

Leila McKenzie-Delis, Founder Dial Global,
Chair of the CEO Impact Council &
Author of the CEO Activist, Putting the S in ESG

1

THE JOURNEY FROM DIVERSITY AND INCLUSION TO BELONGING

Diversity and Inclusion continues to be a topic that is at the forefront of discussions at top levels of many organizations. We are all aware of the work that has been and is being done in this space and the developments in the area over the last 10 years or so. But whilst we have achieved a lot in the inclusion space and brought key challenges to the boardroom table, there is still something lacking.

When I speak to staff within organizations many talk about the initiatives, they see their organizations championing and implementing, but they don't always feel that these initiatives talk to them or have an impact on their sense of inclusion within the workplace. This continues to be a trend within many organizations and despite all the great efforts there still seems to be a gap in achieving success in the inclusion space.

In order to understand how we shift from diversity and inclusion into Belonging and what the latter really means, we must dissect our current efforts and begin to understand the challenges we face and how we can be innovative in creating a sense of belonging that many of our staff desire.

When I say diverse talent or underrepresented talent, what does that mean? Do we immediately think Gender, Race, Disability and Sexual Orientation? If so, we must ask ourselves, is that the right definition of diversity? It is a fact that no one person is one element of diversity. Intersectionality means we have multiple layers to our unique authentic identities, some of which are visible, and others are non-visible.

When defining what diversity is we need to consider all elements of diversity like neurodiversity, age diversity, socioeconomic background, cultural diversity and lived experiences. We must do this to truly understand everyone's unique authentic identities especially if we are going to create a workplace in which everyone feels they can be themselves and belong.

Diversity is also not about one group, nor does it limit it to one. Many times, you hear the words 'diverse talent' in reference to traditional areas of diversity. However, to be able to create a culture of inclusion and one that values all elements of diversity we must ensure the conversation includes everyone because diversity is not limited to one group but is about all of us and every single person has elements of diversity.

What is important is that we also acknowledge and understand local context when it comes to diversity. Even though inclusion is something that is universal, diversity is not, and so, we must understand local nuances when it comes to diversity. For example, in India nearly everyone would be what the UK or US would describe as a person of colour or someone who is an ethnic minority, however in India, where majority of the population would fit this element of diversity, we need to look further and understand local nuances like the caste system, religion or social economic background.

When looking at local nuances, we should also consider how who is underrepresented can shift or change. For example, would a straight white man in India be a minority or would they be part of the majority? They would be a minority when it comes to race but might still be a majority when it comes to gender. Therefore, it is fundamental that organizations understand what diversity means in different global regions if they are going to drive efforts that are meaningful in different countries.

Over my career, I have heard many people talk about inclusion and many organizations even shift the conversation from Diversity and inclusion to inclusion and diversity with the view that if they get inclusion right, they will automatically achieve diversity. This is true to some extent; however, we need to understand what inclusion means and if it really is the end goal for us.

To this, let me present you with an example, if let's say we have a team that is predominately men and a woman joins the team, could we say we now have diversity (and inclusion) on the team? I would argue we don't. Because unless the women can be her true self, have trust and psychological safety to share different views, ideas and opinions, she will have to adapt to the group thinking within the team, which will not result in any benefits for an organization or the individual from a diversity and inclusion perspective, in fact it might do the very opposite and result in a lack of it.

Many times, it is also misunderstood that being included, by itself, will result in greater diversity or benefits to an individual and or organization. However, just being included doesn't drive benefits from a diversity perspective. To truly benefit from diversity, we must create cultures that embed the principles of inclusion and belonging by creating environments where differences are celebrated, not just tolerated.

This brings me, quite nicely, onto Belonging and why it is such an important area of D&I. So where do we start? Well, we need to work on the 'I' in D&I to achieve the 'B' in Belonging. Let me explain this better: We have strengthened diversity to a certain extent by recognizing that people are different and that individuals may have different characteristics that make up who they are. As organizations and D&I teams, we have been working hard on creating a truly inclusive workplace that is reflective of the diversity we see, but how will we know when we are truly inclusive? Well, that's where belonging comes in – the output of true inclusion is a sense of belonging for all our staff.

You might be wondering how we can personify belonging, right? Well, I believe it is the feeling that you can be yourself within a workplace and that you can bring as much of your authentic self as you want to bring to work. Belonging is not a new concept and one we have all grown up feeling at some point in our lives. We might have had that sense of belonging when with our families, when we were part of a sports team or even a group of friends.

If we reflect on that time, what you will find is that when you belonged, you could be yourself. You could contribute 100% and more importantly you didn't have imposter syndrome, have to code switch, or the need to put on a façade in order to fit in – you could just be 'you'. And this is what we need to try to achieve within our workplaces if we are truly going to create work environments that are inclusive and more importantly successful in everything we do.

There is also a lot of research in this space, and it all suggests that not only is belonging something we all crave for, but it is something that, if we achieve, can also unite all our people. Belonging is a concept that every single person within our organization can back and feel that they are a part of, creating a sense of belonging for all.

In fact, in the context of work, a piece of research by EY showed that when people feel like they belong, they are more productive, motivated and engaged as well as 3.5 times more likely to contribute to their full, innovative potential. Therefore, it is not only great for our people, but it is great for our businesses.

WHO DOESN'T WANT A SENSE OF BELONGING, RIGHT?

It unites the efforts of D&I to create a truly inclusive workforce that can not only address some of the age-old challenges we face in the D&I world but help support the advancements of our efforts to achieve the success that we are all after without leaving any group behind and allowing every single person to feel that they can be themselves at work.

Let's look at some of the efforts we see in the space of diversity, inclusion and belonging (DIB) and how we could apply a different approach to them to achieve that sense of belonging for individuals and ultimately the desired outcomes for us as businesses which will drive long-term sustainable change.

When we talk about our efforts, do they resonate with everyone? How many initiatives do you have within your organizations that are aimed at only women, or only people of colour or only at the LGBTQ+ community or people with disabilities? Are these really working or are we falling into the trap of assuming firstly that one element of diversity is important to an individual and, even worse, assuming all their needs are based on that one element of diversity.

I remember at one of the organisations I worked for, we ran a Women's Leadership programme for mid-career-level women and the intention of the programme was to support their development into senior leadership positions. However, the programme's focus areas were based on stereotypes. We had modules that talked about women being more confident or how women can create more presence within the workplace but all the characteristics we tried to introduce as solutions and interventions were masculine traits.

Therefore, a question arises around how we can support unrepresented groups without ending up having a negative impact on the very groups we want to create more inclusion for. Much of my recent work has focused on understanding where the challenges lie to creating inclusion and that is not around 'fixing' certain groups but more so around how we drive that sense of belonging across our organizations and people in order to create environments that drive change.

This doesn't require us to treat diverse groups differently but more around how we create processes and environments that have DIB built into all elements of the processes as opposed to separate initiatives. Let's take the example of the Women's Leadership Programme, which I mentioned above, and apply this concept. We have instead focused on adapting the content of our main leadership programmes to be more inclusive, as opposed to creating separate programmes based on stereotypes.

This would not only lead to wider inclusion but also then organically allows underrepresented groups to feel like they are part of the organization and not singled out for their differences, instead included in the main stage which is welcoming and inclusive of all, yet values diversity through creating equity. Remember we need to stop trying to fix groups of people but focus on fixing the systems around them that are broken.

PSYCHOLOGICAL SAFETY

Another key element to creating belonging is psychological safety for everyone. Many times, when we speak about psychological safety the conversation focuses on creating a safe space for a particular group, but we should instead be focusing on creating psychological safety for everyone through creating working environments where we can talk, explore and learn more about each other and where making a mistake doesn't mean that you are immediately cancelled, or ridiculed but instead where we can grow and learn from each other in a safe environment.

To create environments of psychological safety, we must show vulnerability, a readiness to actively listen and more importantly respect differences. With focused intention, openness and some specific actions, we can help create positive experiences of belonging for ourselves and others.

After the murder of George Floyd, the organization I worked for at the time was very keen to host 'listening sessions' globally in an attempt to create a safe space for honest conversations and better understand the challenges and experiences of their Black employees. I spoke to our leaders about the importance of active listening – that going into these conversations was not about trying to problem solve, get defensive or throw blame but instead to listen, understand and then work together on finding solutions to the challenges our Black colleagues faced.

Many leaders were worried about the language they should use or if they knew enough to be able to have this difficult conversation. Some leaders didn't even see the issues faced by the community and believed we were already diverse and inclusive and therefore didn't need to do these sessions. What was clear was the need to create an authentic conversation with psychological safety for our Black staff and our leaders to be able to have these important conversations in an honest way.

A critical element of the conversations was the foundations we created for the conversations which required everyone to value intent, context and impact. Which was all about the fact that if someone's intent is positive in the right context, but the impact of their words is negative, we should correct, educate and learn. However, if someone's intent is negative within the context of the conversation, then the conversation cannot advance or have the psychological safety that is necessary to learn and grow.

The sessions were successful and we were able to make a lot of progress towards understanding and working together on creating more racial equity in our global workforces through a shared vision of what needed to be done and although everyone didn't agree with every solution or viewpoint, a clear way forward was determined that involved everyone and valued different views and insights, that ultimately supported us in doing a better job.

Another important factor to move on the journey from diversity and inclusion to belonging is the importance of inclusion within our inclusion efforts. Many times, our offerings within the D&I space speak to select groups of employees and although our intentions are positive, they end up creating an 'us and them' culture which goes against the very ethos of DIB and doesn't support the overall culture of inclusion that we want to achieve.

I remember working for a company where we had emergency childcare as an initiative which was an offering designed to help support inclusion by offering a service that our staff could use if their childcare fell through, and they needed support. The service provided up to 4 days emergency childcare for parents through a nursery or babysitter. It was a great initiative that supported working parents but felt exclusive to one group and not inclusive of those who might not have kids.

When we initially looked at it, the view was that it was there to create equity for parents and therefore it was great, which it was but we decided that we needed to explore if more could be offered to help reach more of our staff. So, we asked the providers of the service, if they could broaden their offering to cover those that might not have kids but have elderly parents who might need emergency backup care or those that might not have kids or elderly parents but might need it for a partner.

This helped us create more inclusion through a service that was intended for one group but could easily be adapted or changed to reach a wider audience of our staff and be more inclusive of others. In our pursuit for inclusion, we can sometimes get so focused on addressing specific challenges that we forget to think about how we can be more inclusive within our very inclusion efforts that we design.

EQUALITY OR EQUITY?

The concepts of equity and equality are foundational to understanding fairness within inclusion efforts. While the two terms are often used interchangeably, they represent distinct approaches to addressing disparities. Recognizing the difference between equity and equality is crucial for designing systems that support all individuals effectively.

Equality refers to providing everyone with the same resources or opportunities, based on the assumption that everyone starts from an equal place and requires the same level of support. While this approach appears fair, it can inadvertently perpetuate inequities because it ignores systemic barriers, historical disadvantages and individual differences. For instance, imagine three individuals of varying heights trying to watch a baseball game over a fence. If each person is given an identical box to stand on, the tallest person can easily see over the fence, the medium-height person can barely see, and the shortest person still cannot see at all. Equality in this scenario fails to achieve fairness because it assumes that identical solutions work for everyone, without addressing their unique needs.

In contrast, equity focuses on providing resources and opportunities tailored to individual needs, aiming to level the playing field. It acknowledges that different people face different challenges and adjusts support accordingly. Returning to the baseball game example, equity involves giving resources in proportion to need: the tallest person receives no box, as they can already see over the fence; the medium-height person is given one box, which allows them to see comfortably; and the shortest person is given two boxes, enabling them to see as well. By addressing individual needs, equity ensures everyone has an equal opportunity to participate.

The key difference between equality and equity lies in their focus and outcomes. Equality emphasizes sameness, applying identical resources universally, which can often maintain or exacerbate disparities. Equity, on the other hand, prioritizes fairness by allocating resources based on specific needs, striving to eliminate barriers and create truly equal outcomes.

While thinking of inclusion we need to understand that there isn't always the same level of equity for all groups within the workplace, which means an equality approach alone will not have the impact we want.

Another way to understand equity versus equality is in the context of the COVID-19 pandemic. I remember when we went into lockdown during the pandemic, many organizations wanted to ensure their businesses continued to run remotely and they worked tirelessly to provide their staff members globally with various resources from chairs, desks, keyboards to specific monitors for some teams to ensure everyone was still able to complete the tasks they needed to. The organizations I worked for at the time gave everyone the option to utilize up to €1000 to purchase any equipment they needed to be able to complete their role from home.

This was a great example of equity. If we had taken an equality approach to working remotely, we would have sent everyone the same keyboards, monitors, cables, chairs, etc. and assumed that it would be enough for them to work from home. Of course, we know it would not have been, and instead, this approach would have resulted in many employees not being able to work due to their specific access needs. So, taking this example and applying it to our other efforts, we must understand that everyone is not at the same starting line and will need different levels of support, to reach the same finish line.

5 STRATEGIES TO JUMPSTART YOUR LONG-TERM INCLUSION TRAINING JOURNEY

As we explore ways that we can create workplaces that are inclusive, diverse and where people have a sense of belonging, we must look at learning within inclusion and how to create learning which has the intended impact, is authentic, drives meaningful change and most importantly is distributed across the entire organization, regardless of seniority. Learning takes a multi-dimensional approach from traditional learning, experiential learning and self-taught learning, and the same should be applied to our learning at work.

From Harvard research to diversity and inclusion articles, wherever you look, you'll find articles proving that one-off unconscious bias and diversity trainings do not work. Yet many organizations continue to try to deliver the cliché half-day 'Unconscious Bias' training with the hope that it will fix biases within the workplace and create inclusion or, even worse, the sessions are used as a punishment for when something goes wrong within a team or department.

The reality is that one-off half-day training courses do not embed change and whilst they might appear to change behaviours, they only do so for a short period of time. Real change happens over time not over half a day. Research has proven that individuals will revert to 'normal' after a few months, weeks or even hours. Inclusion training by itself also (ironically) runs the risk of alienating people as there is sometimes a feeling that training points fingers at certain groups or people who are at a certain level (mainly at the basic level) in their understanding of D&I.

However, this doesn't mean we should shy away from training or learning around D&I, in fact we should do the opposite instead creating a journey of learning that creates behavioural change and supports people regardless of their level/rank, or understanding of the simple concepts of D&I. Just as racial justice and education is not a pit stop but a journey, we should view D&I training in the same way – especially if we are going to have a long-term impact on creating true inclusion in the workplace.

Having worked with companies like EY, The Telegraph. adidas and more recently, in Warner Bros. Discovery as Chief Inclusion Officer, I've observed patterns and strategies that have helped employees to embark on a mindful journey towards inclusion and create long-term sustainable change through creating a road map of continuous learning activities, that supports teams across any business.

For corporate inclusion training to be effective, it has to be both long-lasting, encourage a change in behaviour and more importantly it has to be relevant to each and every team across your business, for it to add value and support an organization's D&I ambition.

Therefore, the first criterion for any training to work is to make it part of your employees' career journey with you. Ask yourself what would work best for your environment, because just like everyone's educational journey is different, so is every individual's journey within a company. Here are five strategies that I've applied working with global companies and the best-practices we've brought in that will hopefully jumpstart a sustainable inclusion journey for your teams too:

1. Everyone learns differently

We need to remember that everyone learns differently. Not everyone consumes knowledge through traditional taught learning. Some prefer visual learning, some articles and some team exercises. To make your inclusion training effective for every single one of your employees, involve diverse learning styles into your training – this includes classroom, self-taught or experiential learning.

Whilst, during the lockdown, training might have looked like a combination of pre-class learnings through videos, articles or podcasts followed by team exercises over virtual platforms, in a life post-COVID, training can also include experiential learning that provides employees with actual experiences like visiting a community organisation that supports underrepresented groups or attending a cultural event, as opposed to traditional classroom based learning, to give them actual experiences that are different to what they would otherwise experience.

2. Remove Hierarchy

For inclusion training to work, every single person in your team must be involved in the learning experience equally. There shouldn't be a difference between the training material your board members, corporate or retail staff receive – your inclusion training must be inclusive of all staff.

As soon as you differentiate between levels, departments or environments, you will lose message consistency and learning effectiveness. This also means the executive team should be part of the learning sessions just like everybody else. Enable different team members to volunteer to lead team learning sessions, so that every single person feels responsible to lead a topic and promote conversation, rather than one person leading and others listening. This encourages accountability as well and reinforces the fact that there is no hierarchy in learning about D&I.

At one of the organisations I worked for, we put these principles in play and designed a global learning programme, creating a 'culture of inclusion' team workout. In a team workout, just like in any sport when teams get together to practise and strategize gameplay, you can support each other's weaknesses, learn from each other's strengths and come together to perform at your best as a team and ultimately, play at your best.

Most of the time, unconscious bias or diversity training is not effective, because it is aimed at individual learning. To change behaviours in the long run, both within and across teams, you should create a sequence of training that involves everyone regardless of level or rank. For instance, at one of the companies I worked for, we separated the corporate inclusion training into pre-work, live exercises and post-work. The most important part of the journey was to learn with each other during the live exercises.

This gave us all a chance to be open and transparent in a safe space and for this to work, psychological safety was crucial. Having an environment where each member of a team understands that it is safe for interpersonal risk-taking is so imperative. It will allow you to create opportunities and an environment where everyone feels comfortable to learn, share and discuss and which then will allow teams to openly address unique challenges they face in their working environment with each other.

3. Extend Your Training Time-Period

Think about studying any module at school or University. It usually takes a few months to understand the principles, right? Similarly, to enable long-term behavioural change – you'll need to span your inclusion learning over a period. Training should be a journey from anywhere between 6 months to 24 months to truly start to embed inclusive behaviours effectively.

The intention is to get people into the habit of learning. You don't want to start and stop at the basics of what diversity means but address different diversity dimensions at team levels and double down your efforts on specific areas of diversity. This creates an environment for teams to understand that learning goes on beyond just an hour. Learning shouldn't stop, it should be a continuous process and one that is tailored at a team level.

4. Diversify Your Content

When creating the content around your team's learning, use a lot of open-source learning elements such as articles, TED talks, exercises and gamification. D&I is a complex topic, with many different opinions, experts, views and perceptions. Rather than finding 'the perfect' solution, bring in diverse viewpoints including those different or opposing to yours to truly create meaningful conversations. This prompts dialogue and conversation. You want also to ensure that you don't just focus on scholarly education, but you bring in the reality of the world that you operate in.

Diversifying content in inclusion training is essential for creating material that resonates with a wide range of participants and effectively fosters inclusion. A one-size-fits-all approach can inadvertently alienate employees, overlook cultural nuances or fail to address specific challenges faced by different groups. Tailoring content ensures that inclusion training is not only relevant but also impactful, addressing the unique dynamics of varied workplace demographics and environments.

Inclusion training should reflect the realities of its audience, acknowledging the diversity within the workforce. For instance, a training programme for a global organization should include examples and scenarios drawn from multiple cultural and regional contexts, catering to varied workplace norms and systemic challenges. This approach fosters a sense of belonging by ensuring that participants feel seen and understood, enhancing their engagement and connection to the material.

Intersectionality must also be a cornerstone of inclusion training. By considering the compounded experiences of individuals who belong to multiple groups – such as women of colour or LGBTQ+ individuals with disabilities – training programmes can provide a nuanced understanding of inclusion. Without this, training risks oversimplifying or ignoring the complexities of discrimination and privilege.

Empathy-building is another critical outcome of diversified content. Sharing stories and narratives from underrepresented groups – such as an employee with a disability navigating workplace barriers or a religious minority seeking accommodation – humanizes inclusion concepts. This exposure encourages participants to consider perspectives beyond their own and challenges stereotypes.

Diversified content also helps avoid tokenism and oversimplification. When inclusion training focuses solely on one demographic issue, such as gender diversity, it risks diminishing the importance of other dimensions of diversity. A comprehensive approach ensures that all forms of inclusion are valued, maintaining the training's credibility and authenticity.

5. Everyone Owns Learning

Most diversity training is led by experts, and teams simply listen in. Instead, opt for all team members to be involved with different elements to put the accountability on everyone throughout the journey. This way you embed personal accountability for every person on a team and truly accelerate learning and self-reflection. Create roles for different team members in each training session, because if you just listen, you don't learn, you need to actively participate.

If you have to lead something, you embrace it and turn up with a personal sense of responsibility to make it meaningful. Your goal is to create a culture of training & learning that is fostered and spans way beyond the diversity training itself and allows D&I learning to become a natural habit beyond the sessions.

Inclusion training will continue to be an important part of any organization's learning journey towards creating inclusive practices, environments and teams. It is vital that we create a sense of belonging for all our staff and an environment in which we can all learn and grow together and create more equity and inclusion for all. Therefore, getting it right is hugely important to embed and champion true authentic change.

At one of the organisations I worked at we put these principles in play and designed a global learning programme, creating a culture of inclusion – team workout, because, if you want to run any race or take part in any sports, even the top athletes, the ones that are the best at their game work to broaden their capabilities and strengthen their skills. In a team workout, just like in any sport when teams get together to practice and strategize gameplay, you can point out each other's weaknesses, learn from each other's strengths and come together to perform at your best as a team and ultimately, play at your best.

Training should always be an ongoing effort. Learning is continuous. To be successful as a company, you need to embed learning in the long run and allow different teams to learn at their individual pace and after they have learnt the basic elements of D&I, teams can then double down on where the gaps are within their teams and continue their D&I inclusion journey.

2

WHAT TO FOCUS ON IN AN EVER-EVOLVING SPACE

The space of inclusion has continued to evolve over the years with the focus shifting from diversity to an understanding that inclusion and equity need to be achieved in order to achieve more diversity and ultimately a sense of belonging for all. I can remember when I started my career in this space over 20 years ago. Success in diversity was seen as handing out a few balloons, pens and mugs at an event to communities.

Much of this stemmed from a lack of understanding around what needed to be done, what to focus on and ultimately a fear of authentic engagement and a focus on what was the easiest way to tick a box. This approach was not only meaningless but actually did the opposite of what we had set out to achieve and instead divided and created a lack of trust with communities we wanted to engage with.

Since then, we have come a long way and many organizations have shifted their approach from diversity just being a buzz word to acknowledging and valuing diversity by actively working to create more equitable and inclusive environments for everyone, focussing on intersectionality, systemic change and genuine authentic allyship and leaderships.

However, when working on identifying what areas of diversity and inclusion you should focus on, many organizations tend to take a number of predictable approaches that either don't work or don't have the longevity that is required to drive long term meaningful change that is sustainable, adaptable and engaging for all members of an organization. Let's break these down to understand the challenges, limitations and opportunities that each one of the traditional diversity strands can present.

GENDER EQUITY

One of the most common approaches many organizations tend to go with is to work on gender because it is either perceived to be the easiest to tackle or one, they feel most comfortable with. Of course, working specifically on gender has its advantages. Organizations that are global can work on gender across regions as an area of focus to drive their global inclusion efforts, however it is important to remember that even though gender will seem like something that can be applied globally, when it is layered with intersectionality and local nuances, the efforts needed to advance inclusion will end up being very different in each country and region.

For example, you could decide that your areas of focus will be gender globally and to advance equity and inclusion you will run a women's leadership programme to help support them to advance their careers within your organization. Firstly, the assumptions that we need to fix women not the environments they are in, is flawed but for arguments sake, let's say that you run the programme with positive intent.

One of the biggest challenges is that you are assuming that what is limiting women's progression globally is the same. Now, of course, there are certain things that research tells us impacts women's careers globally and these can be used to develop a programme that will help them overcome these challenges, however it would be naïve for us to assume that all challenges women face are universal or to not consider the intersectionality that each woman would have.

Let's take for example women from certain ethnic backgrounds or even from certain countries that might have communities, or individuals, who view the role of women in a specific way. Those women will not only have to contend with the challenges that women generally face but might also have to battle cultural challenges and the views of the role of women both in and outside the workplace. This will present the need for additional layers of support, understanding and development for organizations to consider for the programme to be impactful.

Another example I have come across many times through this generalization of gender globally is the notion that if one woman can make it, so can another. I can't name the number of times I have worked for organizations that have touted their senior female leaders as proof that any women can succeed within an organization, almost as a showcase to say that there are no challenges or barriers within our organization for women.

The challenge with this (and I have heard this firsthand from numerous women) is that the generalization that is placed on women again misses out on the intersectionality that is present for women and this approach puts emphasis only on gender and not on other elements of intersectionality. For example, if these senior women who are showcased as successes for organizations don't have young families, behave like the male leaders in the attributes they display, are ready to sacrifice many elements of their identity to achieve success, then that is not a reflection of success for other women within those organization who might hold other elements of their identity as a key component of who they are and are not willing to compromise on their authentic selves.

Many diversity efforts that are focused on gender take a very stereotypical view of what is needed to support the advancement of equity and inclusion for women in the workplace, like the notion all women need more confidence, or women need to be stronger leaders. These very statements are problematic because not only do they make assumptions that all women lack certain attributes but also emphasize that male qualities are needed to be successful. This in the long term has the opposite impact and only supports a certain kind of woman to progress in the workplace, which defeats the very purpose of inclusion.

WHAT ARE OTHERS IN OUR INDUSTRY DOING?

The other trap many organizations fall into is trying to compare themselves to others within their industry by basing their focus areas on what they see their competitors doing. This approach has many flaws as it assumes that your competitors are doing a great job or the areas that they have decided to focus on are the right ones for your organizations because others 'like us' are doing this so it must be right.

The question we must ask ourselves is whether the approach within our industry is the right one and if so, is it having the desired success. Focusing on an industry approach can be misleading as it makes a number of assumptions that the challenges within inclusion are industry-specific as opposed to more nuanced for each organization. Don't get me wrong, I do believe every industry has their own unique challenges, however by focusing on industry-specific challenges we miss out on a critical element, which is understanding our own unique challenges and opportunities.

By focusing on industry-specific challenges, I have seen organizations shift their focus from championing inclusion to focusing on only being better than their competitors as a factor to measure success, of course healthy competition is great, even in the inclusion space. However, when that becomes the only reason for your efforts then it results in performative inclusion efforts and actions as opposed to real meaningful change that your staff want to see you engaging in.

I remember one organization where I wanted us to report our ethnicity pay gap which refers to the difference in average pay between different ethnic groups in a particular country or region. It is a measure of inequality in the workplace, where individuals from certain ethnic backgrounds may face lower pay and fewer opportunities for career advancement compared to others.

When I approached the leadership at the company to discuss reporting the ethnicity pay gap voluntarily at the time, as there was no requirement to report it like the gender pay gap in the UK which had a requirement, I was asked if any of our competitors reported it and if so, what their ethnicity pay gaps were and if we were better than them.

I wanted us to report on the ethnicity pay gap not to be better than our competitors, but to create transparency within our organization and with our ethnic minority colleagues. By understanding what biases, discrimination and structural inequalities existed within our workplace, for example, individuals from certain ethnic groups may face barriers in accessing education and training, performative diversity and pointed the lack of interest the organization had had in the past on racial equity – which was evident by the lack of Black representation the organization had.

As a result of the staff calling us out, the organization had to do a lot of backtracking and eventually had to make a public statement to apologize for the lack of genuine effort as well as implement several costly diversity actions to try to address the lack of investment in racial equity over the years and even then, the staff were not convinced that the organization truly cared as it was seen as the company only invested in racial equity because they were 'called out'.

The other challenge with this approach is the difficulty with truly being able to implement long term sustainable change. One-off actions that are usually the result of jumping from diversity area to area are quick fixes, like a band aid or plaster. They only fix an issue temporarily and superficially, usually causing more damage than good and many times creating additional challenges for organizations.

A further danger of this approach is that you can end up focusing on an element of diversity that is not a challenge for you or is not relevant, which can in turn lead you down the wrong path and alienate other diversity groups within your organization who might as a result of your efforts feel that they are not relevant or important for your organization which could also lead to a divide amongst different groups as they might feel that they are competing with each other.

During the time of BLM, many organizations focused only on the development and support of Black staff and as important as this was, focusing solely on one group of people alienated many others who felt left out of the conversations. The approach also resulted in organizations applying the US version of racial equity globally. This didn't always land well as the experiences of Black staff globally were different, for example when you look at many of the Black African communities in a country like the UK. They did not come to the UK as slaves but as economic migrants or skilled communities of doctors, nurses accounts to name a few.

There were also other regions that didn't have the same representation of the Black Community like the US did. I remember delivering a US-focussed diversity message to our staff in China around BLM and the importance of recruiting more individuals

may be subjected to stereotyping and discrimination
hiring process, or may experience limited opportuniti
progression. If we truly understood this, we could ch
change that was needed.

Instead the whole focus shifted not only to whethe
our industry were reporting their ethnicity pay gap b
we could do to make ourselves look better rather than f
addressing how we promote diversity and inclusion in
place, implement policies and practices that support c
gression for individuals from all ethnic backgrounds, and
equal access to education and training opportunities,
we could promote greater transparency around pay an
progression.

FLAVOUR OF THE MONTH APPROACH

In recent years, one of the favourite approaches of organi
is to go with the 'flavour of the month' approach. This is ba
where organizations focus on an element of diversity that is
ing at a point in time. This has been even more evident in
years with the #Me-too movement and Black Lives Matter.
both events showcasing how organizations jump from one
sity area to another based on what is trending.

There are a number of challenges with this approach, first
doesn't come across genuine and furthermore it can be very diffi
to showcase to your workforce that you really care about a top
you move with trends as opposed to authentic engagement. A gr
example of this was during the Black Lives Matter movement t
had so many companies jumping on the band wagon out of fe
of not doing anything as others were doing something. Majority
the efforts were seen as performative inclusion by many.

Employees were quick to call out organizations for this an
highlight the lack of genuine effort. I remember working with a bi
brand that decided to change their website and social media pages
straight away after the murder of George Floyd to say, 'Black Lives
Matter', to somehow showcase their support and care for racial
equity. Within hours, our staff called us out for what was rightly

from the Black community. Many of the staff in China did not understanding how they could achieve this due to the low representation of the Black community in the country. On reflection a better message would have been one that acknowledged the US specific challenges with racial equity for the Black community, followed by the global challenges with Racial Equity and then a local focus.

VISIBLE VERSUS NONVISIBLE

Organizations also tend to focus on elements of diversity that are visible like gender, visible disabilities, race and ethnicity, as they are easier to identify visually and therefore automatically there is a perception that these areas are more important and easier to focus on and that focusing on them will show a clear commitment for organizations in their drive for inclusion.

Although focusing on visible elements of diversity might be great for the pictures in the annual diversity report or shareholder briefing, where you can show a collage of the diversity of your organization. The truth is that focusing only on visible elements of diversity can create a real lack of inclusion for those that don't have visible elements of diversity and furthermore make your efforts seem performative.

However, the most important thing to remember is that no person is one thing, no one is only one element of diversity and even when we focus on visible elements, we don't truly capture the unique identities of everyone. Let me give you a personal example, many organizations over my career have placed me in the race box or only talked to me about race as they can visibly see that I am from an ethnically diverse background, and they assume it's the most important thing to me or the challenge that I face when it comes to inclusion.

The truth is that is far from reality and although race can and has been an area that has been personally challenging for me during my early career, my current biggest challenge is trying to be a present father to two young kids (a 7-year-old and 5-year-old), however no one talks to me about that as they can't physically see it or they assume that it's not important to me as a man.

I have also found that during my career, race has been the constant visible element, but other areas have also become important like being a parent, having nonvisible disabilities, being neurodiverse and the list goes on. I find that the only way we can truly embed change and focus on the right areas within diversity is when we don't focus only on the visible but understand the multiple layers of each staff members unique authentic identities that also include nonvisible elements of diversity.

GENUINE INTENT AND IMPACT

If you have ever asked yourself what you should focus on when it comes to inclusion or gone with the safe bet of focusing on an area that works for you or defaulted to focusing on a current diversity challenge because you see others doing that or you perceive it to be the right thing to do, then you are not alone. Many organizations are faced with these challenges daily but to truly drive change, you must take a unique approach that works for you, rather than one of the above.

So, the question is, what do you do then? Well, the best way is to drive authentic change while bullet-proofing your organization for any challenges and changes in the diversity world around us. You will at times need to double down your efforts in a certain area of inclusion but the key is to still ensure you continue to focus on other areas of diversity as well as those that need more attention in order to take a multi layered sustainable approach that will continue to equip you to be proactive and not reactive.

One of the most important things for an organization is to create both equity and equality within the work they undertake in the space of inclusion. You cannot focus on an area of diversity and ignore others or only invest in one area. The best efforts are those that take an equality approach in the investment of all areas of diversity while understanding the importance of creating equity within their drive for equality for those areas of diversity that have traditionally been ignored or not had much investment.

Practically it's about ensuring engagement with all elements of diversity even if an area doesn't seem that important now, it is crucial that our focus remains on the continuous investment of fairness. Not only does this ensure buy in from different groups but if a challenge was to arise in the future your actions will not seem performative but instead will be valued as a continuation or doubling down on previous efforts.

Recently I was speaking to staff during our town hall about our new inclusion strategy and when it came to the questions at the end, one member of staff asked what we were doing about neurodiversity and if it was even an area of focus for our company. Due to our investment in various strands of diversity, I was able to give him some examples of what we had done while also asking him if we needed to do more. This was not only appreciated by him but the wider organization as well, as it showed our genuine care for various topics that matter to different groups within our workforce.

In our focus on what matters it is also important we look at what our unique organizations need by focusing on what the gaps are within our workplace rather than looking at others in our industry. This is especially important to ensure we don't end up investing in a particular programme or initiative that try to address something that doesn't exist and in turn create a diversity gap that never was.

I remember once speaking to a company that wanted to focus on gender recruitment to diversify their workforce and they were celebrating how they had managed to recruit a number of women into HR roles in their organization. This presented a few challenges to me. Firstly, women are generally overrepresented in HR and therefore focusing on this as a win took away from the actual issue the organization had: a lack of women in other departments.

The other challenge of this even from a HR perspective was the lack of intersectionality of the women they recruited. Many of the women were white, straight and privileged and even though many organizations see diversity within their HR teams as a win when it comes to diversity due to the representation of women, it really isn't, as many of the women are homogenous and don't represent the diversity that is present within gender. Therefore, to truly drive change, we must look deeper and challenge ourselves to look at what really needs to change as opposed to what is easier to change.

GETTING COMFORTABLE WITH BEING UNCOMFORTABLE

Sometimes focusing on certain areas of diversity is uncomfortable because we might feel it's too risky or that we don't know enough to truly champion it, or it's not the right time. The truth is we need to get comfortable with being uncomfortable as the ever-changing world of inclusion will continue to present new challenges and opportunities which we will not always fully understand or be comfortable talking about. However, saying nothing or focusing on what is perceived as easier options, will not help drive the change within your organization that your staff want to see.

Over the years, I have seen so many organizations focus on areas that they are comfortable with, which is usually gender. This ends up leaving many of their staff from other diversity categories questioning whether the organization truly cares about wider elements of diversity and ultimately making staff from other groups feel like they don't belong or that their organization doesn't understand their needs.

If we are truly going to drive change, we must focus on the difficult conversations and champion areas of diversity that we might not be comfortable with or have enough knowledge about. Many organizations also shy away from difficult conversations because they feel that by highlighting an area they don't know enough about or haven't done enough in would somehow call them out for a lack of engagement. The truth is not doing anything is not an option and will have a worse outcome in the long run.

One of the organisations I worked for had spent a lot of time focusing on gender and race but completely ignored other elements of diversity in their strategies. This had resulted in them being continuously called out for a lack of engagement in other areas and we found ourselves spending most of our time trying to fight fires when things came up from a lack of engagement with other groups. This prevented us from driving meaningful change within the organization – meaningful change that was much needed.

It was only when we started to broaden our engagement into other elements of diversity that our staff started to not only have confidence in our approach but work with us to drive the agenda forward. This was a great win for the organization as ultimately, we were all rowing in the same direction which resulted in much more positive engagement and change and made everyone feel included in the conversation.

3

DEEPENING YOUR UNDERSTANDING OF INCLUSION

Whenever I speak to individuals about inclusion, one common theme that emerges is the fear individuals have around the topic, the fear of being cancelled or called out. The fear to get it wrong or the fear to ask certain questions. Furthermore, many people feel that education in this space is the responsibility of the organization or the inclusion department. The truth is we all must own our inclusion learning journey and do this without fear but with an open mindset that is ready to learn and grow.

The learning journey around inclusion is a lifelong one and one that requires us to continue to learn and grow our own understanding. Even the greatest of experts and leaders in the space of diversity and inclusion make mistakes if they don't continue to evolve their understanding and knowledge. However, we must note that learning doesn't only take place in the workplace, we must challenge ourselves to learn both in and outside of work if we are going to truly understand.

Learning more about inclusion is not only for those from the majority groups, but also for those from underrepresented groups as for us to truly have meaningful dialogue we all need to learn and grow if we are going to create more equitable workplaces for all. The challenge we face is that society is completely divided and so are our workplaces. You have to pick a side – either the left or the right, there is no middle left in the inclusion conversation. The truth is that the beauty of diversity is that we all think differently and it's ok to have diverse views and still work together to produce exceptional results.

We must also acknowledge and understand that although inclusion is a universal feeling and outcome, diversity doesn't look the same globally and if we are going to learn and deepen our understanding in this space, we must understand the nuances and differences that exist when it comes to diversity from a global perspective in various regions, countries, cities and towns that we operate in. The one-size-fits-all approach doesn't work.

And remember although inclusion learning is fundamental to our growth and understanding, it is only the beginning of the journey to creating inclusion. I sometimes use the analogy that it is like getting your driving license, you have to study in order to pass your theory test, once that's done you have to take lessons with an instructor to put it into practice and to help you prepare for your practical driving test. Once you have done your test and got your license, you can now drive all on your own, but you must remember what you learnt and apply it in your day-to-day driving and of course continuously refresh your learnings as things change!

LEARNING IS AN INDIVIDUAL COMMITMENT

Research has shown that to truly embed diversity and inclusion learning we must focus on learning being a lifelong journey to embed meaningful change. It demands an ongoing, intentional commitment to growth, reflection and education. This approach ensures that inclusion becomes a sustained effort, fostering meaningful and lasting change.

Inclusion is a dynamic field, constantly evolving alongside societal shifts, cultural developments and new research insights. For instance, as awareness around gender identities broadens, individuals and organizations must stay informed to adopt inclusive language and practices that authentically support all employees. Similarly, as the understanding of intersectionality deepens, inclusion efforts must expand to address overlapping systems of marginalization effectively. Staying updated on these advancements requires continuous education and adaptability.

A critical component of lifelong learning involves unlearning biases and challenging assumptions. Unconscious biases, shaped over time by societal norms and personal experiences, require deliberate effort to identify and mitigate. Confronting these biases is not a one-time event but an ongoing process of self-awareness, education and behavioural adjustments.

Embedding inclusion principles into workflows and organizational strategies also necessitates skill refinement and regular practice. Just as professionals hone their expertise in areas like finance or technology, inclusion requires a commitment to learning inclusive leadership, equitable hiring methods and strategies to foster belonging.

To support lifelong learning in this space, individuals and organizations can engage in various activities that promote growth. Participating in inclusion-focused workshops, certifications or conferences allows individuals to learn from experts and peers while deepening their understanding of effective strategies. Engaging with diverse perspectives through books, podcasts and thought leadership from individuals with lived experiences different from their own can also broaden understanding and empathy. Reflection and feedback are equally vital; by evaluating one's inclusion journey and seeking input from colleagues or diverse groups, individuals can identify areas for improvement and adjust their approaches.

Staying informed about current events and societal changes ensures inclusion efforts remain relevant and impactful. Movements like #MeToo or Black Lives Matter highlight systemic inequities that organizations must address to stay aligned with societal expectations. Recognizing inclusion as a lifelong journey fosters a growth mindset, encouraging humility and resilience. By committing to ongoing education and reflection, individuals and organizations embed inclusion as a core element of success, ensuring sustained impact and meaningful change.

Experiential learning is one of the most powerful forms of inclusion learning, we learn best through experiences, and they stick with us for a lifetime. Usually, uncomfortable experiences, which topics around diversity can be for many are the most powerful. If I asked you to reflect on a comfortable experience, how far back can you go? An hour, a day maybe even a month. However, if I asked you to reflect on an uncomfortable experience, I am pretty sure you could go back to your childhood. That's the power of experiences especially when they are uncomfortable.

Self-taught learning is not just beneficial – it's essential. Inclusion is a dynamic and ever-evolving field that requires continuous learning, reflection and adaptation. Relying solely on formal training sessions or organizational-mandated training is not enough to fully understand the complexities of this work. Self-taught learning empowers individuals to take ownership of their personal growth, allowing them to explore a wide range of perspectives, histories and lived experiences that may not be covered in standard training.

When individuals engage in this type of learning, they demonstrate a commitment to personal accountability in their inclusion journey. This proactive approach fosters a deeper understanding of the systemic issues that contribute to inequality and exclusion, as well as the biases that each person may hold. By exploring diverse sources – such as books, podcasts, articles, TED Talks and conversations with people from different backgrounds – individuals can develop a more nuanced and empathetic understanding of the world. This, in turn, enhances their ability to contribute meaningfully to inclusion efforts within their organizations and communities.

GLOBAL VERSUS LOCAL

There are many times that an organization needs to develop its learning from a global perspective to ensure a baseline understanding of what matters to an organization and their focus areas. There are many elements of diversity that can definitely transcend borders like gender which can be viewed from a global perspective, however, to deepen on our understanding it is important that as we advance our efforts and learning we start to understand intersectionality and local differences.

When considering global training, it is important to remember that the training must use language that is globally relevant to your workforce and simple to understand. Many times, we tend to develop global training using complex English words that don't translate well into other languages or using examples within the training that are only relevant to a specific country or region. Of course, there are elements of inclusion training that can be globally relevant but to ensure understanding and impact, local nuances must be built in.

I recently worked with a tech organization that was keen to develop global training on gender equity for their workforce with the ultimate goal of improving representation at all levels within their company. Now we knew that some fundamental elements of creating more gender equity will be the same globally like the importance of pay equity, shared parental leave and encouraging more women to study technology-related subjects to diversify the future pipeline coming into the industry.

However, we wanted to make sure it landed in all the regions that they operated in: Middle East, Europe and Asia and therefore the training started off by creating a global understanding of gender equity and then deepened into local challenges and opportunities. This approach to the training did take longer to create as we ran focus groups, surveys and one-to-one interviews with their female staff in all the regions to better understand their perspectives as opposed to only looking at general challenges within the markets.

By adopting this approach the training not only gave their staff a global understanding of gender equity but also dived deeper into local nuances and as we had used internal research to develop the local element of the training, the content felt a lot more relevant and was more impactful as the stories and examples within the training were of their staff and made all those who went through the training feel a sense of urgency and relevance as it was based on their female colleagues experiences.

When thinking about training globally, it is important to remember that there are different laws in different countries, and some prevent us from delivering certain elements of inclusion training. For example, when it comes to LGBTQ+ training, there are still many countries where it is illegal to be a member of the community and therefore it would hinder us to deliver LGBTQ+ specific training in those countries.

Local relevance ensures that inclusion training addresses the specific challenges, historical contexts and social dynamics of a particular region or community. This makes the training more practical and applicable to the people it aims to serve. Global-only approach risks being too generalized, while a local-only focus might miss broader systemic issues. By combining both, inclusion training can avoid a 'one-size-fits-all' approach, ensuring it is both inclusive and specific.

Understanding Global versus Local nuances is essential for any organization, The Three Colours of Worldview framework from Knowledge Workx is an example of a framework that explores the deep cultural drivers that shape our thinking, speaking and acting. These three drivers – honour-shame, innocence-guilt and power-fear – are central to understanding intercultural communication and behaviour.

The Honour-Shame worldview prioritizes doing what is honourable for one's group, whether family, organization or nation. This worldview is often relationship-driven, where every interaction can affect one's honour and status. In contrast, the Innocence-Guilt worldview emphasizes doing the right thing based on clear rules, agreements and ethics. People with this worldview are driven by the desire to avoid guilt and uphold laws and morals. The Power-Fear worldview focuses on assessing one's position in the hierarchy, with individuals striving to gain power, influence and security within a structured system.

These cultural lenses interact in complex ways. For example, people with an Innocence-Guilt worldview may struggle to understand the concepts of honour and shame prevalent in other cultures. Similarly, those from an Honour-Shame orientation may misinterpret the behaviours of people from an Innocence-Guilt culture who unintentionally bring shame upon themselves. The Power-Fear worldview, common in hierarchical societies, can lead to power struggles where authority figures must decide whether to use their power for good or to instil fear.

The Three Colours of Worldview framework not only helps individuals understand their own cultural preferences but also enables them to engage with others more effectively. This understanding is crucial in diverse contexts like leadership, collaboration and communication. By applying this framework, individuals and organizations can improve cross-cultural relationships, adapt strategies for teamwork and leadership and foster inclusive environments that embrace diverse perspectives.

Incorporating these insights into organizational culture and practices can lead to more effective teams, better communication and stronger relationships in global and multicultural environments. The Three Colours of Worldview tool, along with the Cultural Mapping Inventory (CMi), are great examples of trainings that offer" a structured way to develop intercultural competency and adapt behaviours for successful interactions in both professional and personal contexts.

JUST TALK

Even if you master the art of inclusion learning and have the best trainers in the world, one of the most important elements of learning in this space comes from actual conversations, when people share their personal experiences, challenges and are open to listening actively without judgement. This creates authentic learning and humanizes what people are going through and provides the learner with a real opportunity to understand and learn more about what someone has or is experiencing. When people hear an experience of their colleague, they are more likely to understand and feel an elevated level of empathy.

However, we must be mindful that although many people are more than happy to talk about diversity and their personal experiences, not everyone who is from an underrepresented group is ready to share their experiences and this is ok. Many people don't want to relive the trauma they might have experienced or are just not comfortable to talk about their personal experiences, we need to respect this and not see it as someone being difficult but instead be ready to respect their wishes. It is also important to note that not every underrepresented person is an expert on diversity or your encyclopaedia.

I recently worked with an organization to develop their leadership journey over a period of 12 months so that it was not a one-off training and as part of the journey after each taught element within the modules, the leaders were put in small groups to discuss what they had learnt and share how they could put the learning into practice. This was a powerful way of equipping leaders with not only the knowledge they needed but helping them put that knowledge into practice in a safe space where they could make mistakes, learn and grow.

The feedback from the leaders was overwhelmingly positive, with over 90% saying that the most beneficial part of the learning experience was the group breakouts that not only gave them an opportunity to practise what they had learnt but also helped increase their confidence in the inclusion space through discussions with their peers, which in turn helped them to champion inclusion within their teams with more confidence.

DIVERSIFYING YOUR SOURCES

I have lost count of the number of times someone has asked me 'What are the best diversity and inclusion books to read?' or 'What's the best ted talk to watch?'. Now, of course I am happy to recommend some great work in the space led by amazing leaders like Verna Myers, June Sarpong and Lily Zhang to name a few. But what's important to remember is that when we talk about learning in the space of inclusion, just turning to diversity and inclusion content will only give you one side of the story.

Let me explain, let's say you work in the marketing team and for your job you must do some research on why women might not feel safe travelling alone and your boss has asked that you provide some solutions to the problem. If you only spoke to women, you would of course understand their perspective, what creates fear for them and what would make them feel safer right? This is true; however, I am sure the answers will not all be exactly the same and although they will be talking about the same topic each of their perspectives will differ slightly.

But, if you really want to understand what needs to be done, you would also probably speak to some men, look at some data, maybe even explore some recent cases that might help in improving your understanding. Inclusion work is similar, if you only get your information from one source like diversity experts, you will get the common trends in the space but will not truly broaden your understanding as you would if you also looked at some research from academia, some government reports or case studies.

Another important element of learning is to hear from the other side. This means that not only should we focus our sources of learning on what we want to hear but we must broaden it to capture sources that we might not agree with or don't necessarily share our point of view, this is crucial if we are going to have meaningful conversations and a better understanding of other perspectives. Diversifying your sources of information will also allow you to better understand what needs to be done to bridge the gap between different viewpoints.

WHAT NOT TO SAY?

We have all been in situations when we thought we knew what the right thing was to say and then discovered we were very wrong. It is critical for us to have conversations in the space of inclusion, however it is important to stay authentic, curious and speak without bias or judgement. In many conversations, the biggest challenge we face is perception versus reality. Someone might perceive something, and we might feel the reality is different. This is ok, but we must remember someone's perception many times is based on their lived experience and is their reality, even though yours might be different.

I remember having a conversation with someone once about the police and telling them that every time I get stopped, the police stereotype me and assume my car can't be mine or assume I must be a drug dealer to be driving the car I drive and as a result of this I am defensive and abrupt when I now get stopped by the police. They proceeded to tell me that can't be true and that I can't assume every police officer is bad. Now, of course, I don't think every police officer is bad, but my experiences and perception lead me to respond in the way I do, till I feel that I will be treated fairly, then I let my guard down.

I have heard many leaders over the years trying to justify, become defensive or apologise when it comes to topics around diversity. One example is privilege, whenever I have heard leaders talk about privilege, they either apologize for their privilege or deny they have privilege by justifying it through their experiences growing up which might not have been so privileged. The truth is we need to do neither, no one wants an apology or justification, what people appreciate is when we acknowledge we all have privileges and use them for good to help those that might not have the same privileges.

Active listening is a cornerstone of effective communication in inclusion efforts because it creates a space where all voices are genuinely heard and valued. When individuals engage in active listening, they are not merely waiting for their turn to speak; they are fully present, attentive and empathetic to the experiences and perspectives of others. This practice is crucial in inclusion conversations, where diverse viewpoints, often rooted in different cultural, social, or personal backgrounds, need to be acknowledged and respected. By truly listening, individuals can better understand the unique challenges faced by different groups and are more likely to respond with sensitivity and informed action.

Moreover, active listening fosters trust and collaboration, essential elements in creating an inclusive environment. When people feel heard and understood, they are more likely to engage openly and contribute to inclusion initiatives. This sense of being valued encourages a culture of mutual respect and empathy, which is fundamental to breaking down barriers and building bridges across differences. In the context of inclusion, active listening is not just a skill but a commitment to continuous learning and growth, enabling individuals and organizations to move beyond superficial diversity efforts and towards meaningful, sustainable inclusion.

When engaging with marginalized groups about inclusion, it's crucial to recognize that intent and impact can differ significantly. Intent refers to the motivation or purpose behind your words or actions, while impact is the actual effect those words or actions have on others. Even with the best intentions, your message can still cause harm if it is not communicated thoughtfully or if it fails to consider the lived experiences of those you are addressing. For example, a well-meaning comment meant to express solidarity can sometimes come across as patronizing or dismissive, unintentionally reinforcing the very biases or stereotypes you aim to challenge.

This distinction is vital because marginalized groups often navigate a world where their voices are unheard or misunderstood, and they may be more attuned to the impact of words and actions than to the intent behind them. Acknowledging this difference is key to building trust and fostering meaningful dialogue. It requires active listening, humility and a willingness to learn from mistakes. By focusing on the impact of your words and actions, and not just your intentions, you demonstrate a genuine commitment to inclusion principles and a respect for the experiences of marginalized communities.

LEARNING IS NOT JUST FOR THE WORKPLACE

As a leader, it's important to highlight that inclusion learning extends far beyond the workplace – it's a vital part of our lives that profoundly impacts our personal relationships, community involvement and societal contributions. While the workplace often introduces us to formal inclusion initiatives, the principles of inclusion are universally relevant, shaping how we interact with others, appreciate different perspectives and contribute to a fairer, more equitable society.

Beyond the workplace, inclusion learning cultivates empathy and social awareness, helping us navigate diverse social environments, build meaningful connections with people from various backgrounds and actively challenge stereotypes and biases in our daily lives. Whether we are engaging with neighbours, participating in community events, or having conversations with friends and family, the insights gained from inclusion learning empower us to create more inclusive spaces where everyone feels recognized and respected.

Furthermore, embracing inclusion in our personal lives equips us to be stronger advocates for equity and diversity in the broader society. It drives us to acknowledge and address systemic inequalities in our communities, from supporting inclusive policies to confronting discriminatory behaviours when we encounter them. By incorporating inclusion principles into our everyday actions, we help build a more inclusive culture – not just within our workplaces, but throughout society. This comprehensive approach to inclusion is crucial for creating lasting change and ensuring that inclusion becomes a shared societal value, not just a corporate initiative.

An important element of self-led learning is how you continue your inclusion learning outside of work. If we assume we only must learn for work or within work, then you will never truly be able to drive authentic meaningful change both inside and outside of the workplace. We are all creatures of habit and comfort and if you are anything like me, outside of work you will experience the same things regularly like frequenting your favourite restaurant or attending a particular cultural event because its your culture or a particular music festival because it plays your favourite music. Of course, there is nothing wrong with doing any of the above, however will this really help you to broaden your understanding of other people and their different cultures?

The truth is that it will not, we don't have to give up on what we like but be can try to make an effort outside of work to diversify our experiences, maybe go to a different restaurant and try food you have never tried before or attend a cultural event that is not linked to your culture or if you are feeling even braver you could attend a music festival for music you don't even listen too! These experiences might be uncomfortable, but they will help you learn and grow.

4

INCLUSION STRATEGIES FOR WORKPLACE REVOLUTION

Within many organizations, companies have embedded numerous strategies to drive inclusion. Usually turning to best practices, they might have heard of or seen within other companies or even looking at what others in their industry are doing and trying to replicate those initiatives to try to build an inclusion strategy. The challenge with this approach is that if any of the other strategies were great, we would have already solved for inclusion. Now don't get me wrong, many standard strategy approaches do work, however they are usually not equipped for the long run or to drive long-term sustainable change.

Over the years having created many strategies, from those that are 100 pages long to some only being a few slides. I can conclude that on this topic the attention is not on the detail, it is more important to firstly have a strategy that is fluid and can adapt to the changing nature of the inclusion landscape and one that is embedded across different parts of the business with a shared understanding and commitment to driving meaningful change for the organization.

The best of strategies that I have seen over the years are those that have a few pillars of what the organization wants to commit to when it comes to inclusion and then they are built out by each business unit. This way the onus and ownership of the strategy is not just the inclusion team's but the whole organizations and furthermore it allows each business unit to build the inclusion strategy locally based on the overall inclusion pillars and their business unit's (BU) understanding of what needs to be done to achieve the overall goals.

Even though building a strategy can seem like a huge task, the most important thing is not the strategy itself but the strategy you develop to ensure buy in across the organization. When I worked in the public service sector, there was an over emphasis on getting the inclusion strategy 100% right before we set about communicating it and delivering it to the organization. The truth is, no strategy is 100% perfect and if we wait for the perfect moment or perfect strategy we will be waiting a lifetime. The key is to try and if you get it wrong, learn and try again. No one will ever criticize you for trying and getting it wrong but they will criticize you for not trying.

INTEGRATE INCLUSION INTO YOUR BUSINESS UNIT STRATEGY

Inclusion should not be seen as an add-on or separate initiative but as an integral part of the overall business strategy. This means embedding inclusion goals into the company's mission, vision and values, and ensuring they align with business objectives. Leadership should regularly review inclusion metrics alongside financial performance and make inclusion a key criterion in decision-making processes, from hiring to product development.

When embedding inclusion into a company's strategy, it is important to ensure the language that is used matches the company's language and doesn't seem like an add-on or a nice-to-have statement that doesn't translate to employees as being business critical. Efforts should also be made to integrate inclusion into performance measurable outcomes. This can be done by linking inclusion performance to compensation, promotions and performance reviews. Ensure that leaders are not only committed to inclusion but are also actively involved in its implementation. Regularly reporting on inclusion progress to maintain transparency and build trust within the organization.

A company's core values, principles or mission statement should embody your inclusion language within it if you are going to drive buy-in and critical focus on the topic. Many times, when these elements are being designed for a company, they are done behind closed doors and then presented to your staff with the hope they all align and believe in them. This alone doesn't work; in order to get employees engaged, we have to take an approach that allows them to help build these values, principles or mission, that way they will see it as being something that was built by them for them as opposed to another corporate statement that no one understands.

When I worked for a large newspaper, we decided to refresh our values as the current ones we had, no one really understood and although they were plastered all over our walls, in our canteen and even in the toilets/washrooms. No one really understood what they meant and how they could apply them in their day-to-day roles. Therefore, we embarked on a refresh of the values with the view of building in inclusion into the values as it was a core part of who we were and what we believed in.

In order to build it with our employees we conducted a number of one to one interviews, focus groups and an organization-wide survey to understand what our culture truly was and what our people valued, we then took the feedback and worked with the leadership team to understand what their vision and ambition for the company's growth was and how could we align it to what our people wanted. This helped us create a strategy that reflected both our business objectives as well as our inclusion and cultural objectives and one that everyone bought into.

FOSTER INCLUSIVE LEADERSHIP

Training leaders and line managers at all levels to recognize and address their own biases, lead diverse teams effectively and create inclusive environments is fundamental to creating an inclusive environment and advancing your diversity and equity ambitions. Inclusive leadership involves actively seeking out and valuing diverse perspectives, encouraging open dialogue and ensuring that all team members feel respected and heard. Leaders should model inclusive behaviours and be advocates for inclusion in all aspects of their work if true change is going to be achieved within any organization.

I believe the biggest quality of any good inclusive leader is being an authentic leader and an inclusive leader. That's a phenomenon that wasn't necessarily in place many, many years ago. I still remember being on leadership courses in the past where we were taught that a great leader was considered a strong leader, one who doesn't show weakness, and always has a strong mindset. When we think of a great leader and one that's inclusive, many will say that's a leader that's humble, one that's authentic, that shows vulnerability and doesn't have all the answers. That's what people want to see, a human leader, not a leader that they just see on paper who they can't relate to.

I remember once when I worked for a big consultancy firm, the head of the firm use to write a monthly newsletter in which he talked about business advancements and changes in the industry. The newsletter generally had an open rate of 5–10% and the communication teams had been trying for a number of months to get the open rate higher with the hope of getting more staff members engaged with the newsletter.

I suggested to them to get the leader to be more authentic within the newsletter and to open it with something personal about himself to make him more relatable to the staff. After a lot of backwards and forwards with his teams who were all sceptical about doing this as they felt it would mean him letting his guard down and being vulnerable, which I explained was the exact point, they eventually agreed and I spoke to him. Initially he said to me that he doesn't have anything from a diversity perspective that is personal to him that he can talk about as he is a straight, middle aged, white man.

As we continued to discuss what he could talk about, in conversation he mentioned to me that he had dropped his daughter off to university over the weekend in Glasgow and how stressful it was for him. I was like 'That's it!' and explained to him that he can use that as its personal to him, being a parent is part of being diverse and above all else, it makes him human and relatable to many staff members within the organization. The next newsletter he did went out with an opening paragraph that mentioned he had dropped his daughter to university the previous week.

Just by adding this one element into his newsletter the open rate went from 5–10% all the way up to 30–40%. As I spoke to many of our staff in the coming weeks, the one thing that always came up was how great it was for them to see a leader who was ready to share a bit more about himself, be vulnerable and highlight how he struggles as well, like the rest of us. The leader also found that after he had shared his personal story, he had found that many staff had also approached him and shared their personal experiences and challenges, which in turn had given him great insights into where the barriers were for his people.

ENGAGE AND EMPOWER EMPLOYEE RESOURCE GROUPS (ERGs)

ERGs, also known as Business Resource Groups (BRGs) or Employee Networks, are a great resource for an organization in driving its inclusion objectives and engagement with staff. We should however take a moment to understand what the difference between ERGs and BRGs is as many times the view is that they are the same thing, which is not true. There is a clear distinction between the two and the main one being that one is geared towards employees and supporting them and the other is aimed at the employees supporting the business to achieve its inclusion objectives.

Many times, frustration is created for employee networks when an organization is not clear on which one they need or want. To understand what is best for your organization you must reflect on what your objective for the groups is. ERGs are largely created with three simple objectives: the first is to create a community for an unrepresented identity-based diverse group in order for them to have a safe space and network of individuals who share similar diversity characteristics. The second is to create a community that supports the learning and development of individuals from that group, through development programmes and other initiatives as well as creating a safe space for allies and those who want to learn more about the community can turn to. This learning many times takes the shape of cultural celebrations and events that raise awareness of the community. The final objective is to be a sounding board for the business by providing feedback to the business on specific inclusion issues related to that community.

Although BRGs also provide much of the above, they are different in that they also have a stronger emphasis on aligning their activities with business goals and driving business outcomes. They focus on leveraging the diverse perspectives and insights of their members to influence business strategy, product development, marketing and customer engagement. BRGs aim to contribute to the company's bottom line by using their unique perspectives to tap into new markets, innovate products and enhance customer relations, while also supporting the professional growth of their members. BRGs may also collaborate with business units on market research, product design or community outreach, directly linking their activities to the company's broader strategic goals.

What is important regardless of which you have is how you engage as a company and individuals with them. I have seen many companies with amazing ERGs/BRGs however there is little to no engagement with the wider business, whether it be to drive learning for staff or business objectives. Over the years I have seen some amazing events run by these employee networks to raise awareness of key challenges and opportunities within their communities, one such event has been International Women's day celebrations which are championed by many women's or gender networks within organizations. I have gained so much from these events and insights into what needs to be done to move the needle on gender equity within organizations.

However, every year one of the things I see at these events is that majority of the attendees are women, of course this alone is not a bad thing but where are the men? How are we going to change the landscape if men are not involved or didn't understand the challenges and opportunities that are present to create more gender equity. I have seen some great practices, whereby some employee networks have encouraged each member to bring along a male ally to an event, this resulted in more men learning from the events. Similarly, I have seen other networks go beyond just traditional events and create a safe space where allies and those that want to learn more can come along and ask question in a psychologically safe space, without judgement.

One such event was organized by a Muslim network that was run in an organization that I worked in. They decided to create an event shortly after the Westminster bridge terrorist attacks in London to help their colleagues learn more about their community and dispel myths and stereotypes that the media at the time was creating about the community. Although this was a sensitive topic, what it did was provide colleagues with an opportunity to learn about the community in a safe environment and ask questions without judgement.

Organizations spend a lot of money on consultants to help guide them and support them in better understanding the needs of various groups and support them in developing key strategies to drive change for those groups within their companies. There is, of course, a time that we should use consultants to help get better insights, however is it not better to engage your employee networks who are members of those communities and are within your organization and can provide first hand experiences of what is working, not working and what can be done to change things? Employee networks are able to provide great insights that can better support your inclusion initiatives, plans and lead to more authentic and impactful inclusion efforts that resonate across the entire organization.

I have observed that companies focusing on developing their business for specific identity groups often invest significantly in market research and consultants to gain a deeper understanding of how to effectively engage with these groups or design products and services that meet their needs. This presents an excellent opportunity for organizations with BRGs to leverage these groups for valuable insights and offer their members developmental opportunities by involving them in such projects.

For instance, a drinks company's women's inclusion network played a pivotal role in the development of a new product line. The group provided essential insights into consumer preferences, particularly among female consumers, leading to the creation of a healthier snack option as part of their range. Their contributions were instrumental in tailoring the product to meet the target demographic's needs and preferences, thereby contributing to its success in the market.

A global product manufacturers, African Ancestry BRG, played a crucial role in the creation of a campaign and product line specifically targeting the Black community. The BRG provided insights into the needs and preferences of Black consumers, leading to the development of a range of beauty products that celebrate Black beauty and cater specifically to the needs of Black women. Another example was a Disability Awareness BRG that worked on improving the accessibility of customer service channels for individuals with disabilities. They provided recommendations on features such as text telephone service (TTY) services, screen reader compatibility, and improved website accessibility, enhancing the company's services for all customers.

Although employee networks are voluntary groups, it is important to ensure that they have the resources, support and visibility they need to thrive. Involving them in strategic decision-making, encouraging collaboration across different networks and recognizing their contributions to the company's inclusion goals are fundamentals of a successful employee network.

LEADERSHIP COMMITMENT AND ACCOUNTABILITY

An inclusive leader is someone who not only values diversity but actively creates an environment where all individuals feel welcomed, respected and empowered to contribute their best. They make an effort to understand the unique experiences and perspectives of each team member. This means taking the time to listen actively and with compassion, ensuring everyone feels heard and valued. They are knowledgeable about different cultures, customs and perspectives, and they continuously seek to educate themselves and others. This understanding helps them to create policies and practices that respect and celebrate diversity.

They should also be willing to acknowledge their own biases and limitations, and they actively seek feedback from others. This humility allows them to learn and grow, improving their ability to lead inclusively. They also hold themselves and others accountable for fostering an inclusive environment, setting clear expectations and following through on commitments. They actively promote initiatives and policies that support a diverse workforce and inclusive culture. This advocacy is not just about words, but about taking concrete actions that drive meaningful change.

Leaders must lead by example when it comes to inclusion and demonstrate a personal commitment to diversity and inclusion through their actions and decisions. Through being an active participant in inclusion initiatives, attending events and engaging with diverse groups within the organization. A way leaders can achieve this is by regularly communicating the importance of inclusion in company-wide meetings and be visible in supporting ERGs and other inclusion activities.

Leaders should set clear inclusion goals for themselves, track progress and hold themselves and their teams accountable for achieving them. I recently created a inclusion council within our organization that was made up of the top leaders as we wanted them to utilize their influence in our organization to drive change and an opportunity to put their inclusive leadership to action and lead by example to influence our organization to do the same.

When I was setting up the inclusion council, I didn't want it to be another council that meets every so often and the head of inclusion reports back to the council on progress or initiatives, instead I put the onus on each leader to report back to the council on the progress of their commitments to drive change. The council was created to be a tool to hold leaders accountable to inclusion work; and provided them with a clear structure to be successful. It also allowed them to bring together a working group underneath each one of them that was made up of 6–12 individuals from across their business and included key decision makers, inclusion advocates and representatives of underrepresented groups.

Creating the working groups also helped align all efforts within each BU, moving away from random acts of diversity or pockets of well-intended initiatives that employees were running but didn't have the support or structure to create long-term sustainable change. Being under the command of the leader, ensured that the initiatives had the right support in place as well as backing needed to drive meaningful change. The inclusion team were also on hand to provide data insights, project support and ideas to create clear measurable action plans for each leader commitment.

Each council member was set three business inclusion objectives and three person ones. The idea behind this was that they come up with three commitments for their own BU that they would drive as opposed to replicating the inclusion team objectives. We provided them with diversity data for recruitment, retention, development, progression and exits for each of their business areas to help them identify gaps through the data that they could focus on through their commitments. Every quarter we assess the effectiveness of their inclusion initiatives and adjust strategies based on what is or isn't working and use data to drive decisions and measure the impact of their inclusion efforts. We have also worked with the leaders to use employee inclusion surveys and inclusion audits to identify gaps and areas for improvement, and adjusted their strategies accordingly.

Making inclusion a key component of leadership performance evaluations or pay is one of the biggest drivers of change within any organization. Leaders should be assessed on their efforts to promote diversity and inclusion within their teams. Performance bonuses or other incentives can be tied to achieving inclusion goals, ensuring that leaders are financially motivated to prioritize these initiatives as they would any other business priority within an organization. There is an age old saying 'what gets measured, gets done' and that definitely applies to linking inclusion to performance objectives as this link also creates clear measurable outcomes that will have to be demonstrated by each leader to show that they achieved the objectives ser out in their performance goals.

Now when talking about measurable goals, many companies turn to the end objective immediately rather than the drivers of change. Let me explain: When companies think of goals, they usually go with something like 30% of our leadership will be women or 20% People of colour. As great as these goals might seem they usually lead to leadership behaviour that does the very opposite of what an organization wants to achieve, people scramble around to fill senior roles with women or PoC, sometimes even mandating that a role must only be filled with a diverse hire, which is illegal of course and actually does more harm than good as someone diverse is recruited and not set up for success as people around them think they are a diverse hire, people above them think they are a diverse hire and people below the think they are a diverse hire, which eventually leads to them leaving the organization and you ending up back at square one.

Targets or goals as I like to put them, should be focused on diversifying processes that help support in diversifying the pipelines into leadership. For example, insisting on a certain percentage of diversity in shortlists or creating key development processes for diverse talent that help support their readiness for promotion, with a clear pathway. This can include mentorship and sponsorship programmes that specifically support underrepresented employees, leadership development programmes that focus on building a diverse talent pipeline, and equitable access to training and resources. Regularly reviewing promotion practices is another way to ensure they are free from bias and promote inclusion at all levels.

5

DEVELOPING STRATEGIES THAT IMPACT PROFITABILITY AND CUSTOMER ENGAGEMENT

When it comes to inclusion many times the work is viewed only as an internal element that can support staff and create working environments that are inclusive and where everyone has equitable opportunities. This is of course right and many inclusion efforts in the space are targeted towards supporting the whole employee lifecycle from recruitment, retention, development and progression. However, the truth is, in order to fully reap the benefits of inclusion we must also integrate inclusion into our products and services in order to create organizations that are attractive to both future employees and customers.

There is a lot of research that showcases the business benefits of inclusion despite some arguing that it doesn't impact business, there is plenty of evidence that shows that it does. A recent McKinsey's *Diversity Wins* report highlighted how diverse executive teams significantly boost company profitability, with gender-diverse companies showing a 25% higher likelihood of above-average profitability. The report identifies that genuine inclusivity, where diverse employees experience fairness and belonging, drives sustainable impact in products and services through higher productivity, innovation, creativity and better problem solving as a result of having diversity of though, ideas and lived experiences.

In addition to the profitability link, the *Diversity Wins* report highlights that diversity and inclusion (D&I) drive innovation and resilience, especially in rapidly changing markets. Companies that prioritize inclusion are more likely to attract and retain top talent, improve employee engagement and foster agile decision-making. Despite the benefits, many organizations face challenges with translating inclusion goals into clear actions for their products and services, as inclusion work is seen as an internal facing objectives rather than a business benefit.

As many companies try to reach new markets and new consumer bases, it is evident that the largest growth opportunities lie in diverse consumers and new markets, who traditional might not have been see as a target audience. However, due to movement in wealth and an increased buying power amongst many underserved communities and the rise of wealth in the Middle East, Asia and Africa, there is now more than ever before opportunities to capture new audiences to not only increase profits but to also drive future sustainable growth for companies and organizations. Companies who adapt to this change are more likely to be in a better competitive position then their competitors and others in the market.

As an organization, embedding inclusion into your products and services ensures they resonate broadly and fairly, enhancing both their appeal and usability across diverse populations as well as your traditional consumer base. When inclusion principles are integrated thoughtfully, they foster accessibility, promote inclusivity and align with the unique needs and perspectives of all users, which strengthens customer trust and loyalty. Inclusion-driven products and services are also more likely to empower underrepresented groups, reduce barriers and contribute to positive social change.

There are also numerous examples of how not building in inclusion in the design process of products and services can impact the end design and create products and services that are either not suitable for diverse audiences or culturally inappropriate which can result in reputational risk, losses in profitability and boycotts of your products and services as well as impacting your brand image which can result in a lack of trust in your organization from both employees and customers.

Inclusion in product design is vital for creating products that resonate broadly, meet diverse customer needs and avoid alienating potential users. By prioritizing Inclusion, companies foster a sense of belonging among customers and build trust, especially among underserved or historically marginalized groups. Inclusive product design can expand market reach, boost customer loyalty and enhance brand reputation, positioning companies for long-term success. When Inclusion is overlooked in design, products may inadvertently exclude, frustrate or even offend certain user groups, which can lead to public backlash, decreased sales and damage to brand reputation.

INCORPORATE DIVERSE PERSPECTIVES IN DESIGN

It is important to ensure from the outset, that your product development teams are representative of the diversity of your consumers and that they include voices from underrepresented groups that you want to reach. This diversity within the team can lead to more innovative solutions that resonate with a broader audience as well as better problem solving and mitigation of potential risk in design. Actively seeking feedback from diverse users throughout the development process can ensure different needs, cultures and experiences are considered.

The Deloitte report, *The Diversity and Inclusion Revolution,* argues that embedding D&I directly into core business practices and product design is essential for achieving robust business outcomes. Rather than functioning as standalone HR objectives, Inclusion initiatives should shape how products are conceived, developed and marketed. By integrating diverse perspectives at all stages of product design, companies can create offerings that resonate more broadly, foster customer loyalty and capture new markets. Diverse teams bring unique insights that are especially valuable for innovating solutions that meet a wider range of needs, thus expanding a company's market reach locally and globally and enhancing customer satisfaction.

Deloitte emphasizes the importance of inclusive leadership as the foundation of this transformation. Leaders who champion inclusivity set the tone for product development teams to prioritize accessibility and relevance as a business imperative rather than being seeing as an HR initiative. This mindset enables products to serve more users, which can significantly enhance customer engagement and drive revenue growth. For instance, products designed with accessibility in mind not only benefit users with disabilities but also meet the preferences of a broader user base, thereby increasing potential market share.

The report also highlights that implementing Inclusion goals with clear, measurable outcomes helps organizations assess the impact of their products and services. Tracking metrics, such as the representation of diverse groups among users or the effectiveness of inclusive design features, enables businesses to refine their offerings based on user feedback. Additionally, regular evaluation of Inclusion in product design supports sustainable improvements, as it builds a data-driven approach to inclusivity that adapts to changing customer expectations over time.

It is important to remember that adapting or refreshing product design for one group can have a positive outcome for other groups as well. Many times, when we refresh the design of a product or service, it improves the overall user experience, benefiting a wide range of users. For example, the introduction of dolls with diverse skin tones, facial features and cultural backgrounds has been a successful and growing strategy for many toy companies. In recent years, these companies have expanded their doll offerings to include various skin colours, ethnic backgrounds, body types and even dolls with disabilities. These efforts have been met with positive feedback and increased demand, as more parents and children seek dolls that reflect the world's diversity.

The journey towards diverse dolls began in their 1960s, with the introduction of one of their first Black dolls in the line by a major doll manufacturer. However, it wasn't until the last decade that companies significantly broadened their range to include a wider array of skin tones, hair textures and facial features, representing Black, Asian, Hispanic, Middle Eastern and mixed-race identities, among others. A major turning point came with the introduction of a new product line in 2016, which featured dolls in a range of skin tones, body shapes and even with physical features like vitiligo and prosthetic limbs.

Sales have reflected the demand for this inclusivity. Companies have reported strong financial growth and brand revitalization in part due to the success of these diverse dolls, which have helped the brand resonate with new audiences and reinforce positive cultural shifts. The increase in representation has also been shown to benefit children's self-esteem and social acceptance, as children are more likely to see themselves or their friends reflected in their toys.

For organizations looking to remain competitive, Inclusive product development is a powerful differentiator. As global consumers increasingly expect brands to demonstrate social responsibility, a genuine commitment to inclusion enhances brand reputation, attracts top talent and supports long-term profitability. Deloitte's findings reinforce that when Inclusion is an integral part of both business strategy and product design, companies not only improve internal culture but also drive positive business outcomes and strengthen their market position.

Incorporating Inclusion into product design is more than a trend; it's essential for creating products that reflect the diverse world we live in. Companies that prioritize inclusivity set themselves apart as socially responsible and connected to the needs of a broad consumer base, ultimately enhancing their market competitiveness and sustaining long-term growth. When organizations foster an environment where diverse viewpoints are built into their product design process, they are better equipped to identify potential pitfalls and challenges, thereby minimizing risks. Research indicates that leveraging diversity of thought can lead to a reduction in risk exposure by as much as 30%, as diverse groups are more adept at spotting problems from multiple angles.

DIVERSITY OF THOUGHT

Diverse and Inclusive teams are also more likely to foster innovation. Research shows that organizations with greater diversity are 35% more likely to outperform their less diverse counterparts. This innovative spirit is vital in risk management; as teams brainstorm creative solutions, they can identify and address potential risks before they escalate.

Diversity of thought serves as a counterbalance to groupthink, a psychological phenomenon where the desire for harmony and conformity in a group can lead to irrational or dysfunctional decision-making. By including individuals with varied experiences and opinions, organizations can challenge prevailing assumptions and encourage critical thinking. This dynamic was illustrated in the aftermath of the 2008 financial crisis, where many firms that lacked diversity faced significant risks due to a failure to question their strategies. A diverse team is more likely to challenge the status quo and consider alternative strategies, leading to better risk management outcomes.

Another advantage of a truly Inclusive workforce is that it can provide insights into different markets and customer segments, allowing organizations to identify risks and opportunities associated with emerging markets and different consumer behaviours. One notable example is of a soft drinks manufacturer who have driven this approach in the development of products for local tastes. In Japan, for instance, the company released hundreds of product varieties to suit local preferences, from unique flavours like green tea to seasonal releases that celebrate Japanese culture. This level of customization would be nearly impossible without input from teams who understand the nuances of these markets.

By integrating diversity into product design and market research, the company mitigates risks tied to consumer misalignment, such as the potential backlash from cultural insensitivity or unresponsive product offerings. Diversity within its teams thus acts as a safeguard, ensuring that products and campaigns are well-received and fostering trust in varied markets. Additionally, this approach helps them stay competitive, particularly in emerging markets, where tailored, culturally aligned products enhance customer loyalty and engagement. This proactive alignment with diverse market underscores how diversity not only enhances company culture but also strengthens overall business performance.

REPRESENTATION MATTERS

Research consistently demonstrates that diverse leadership teams are better at decision-making and innovation. For instance, a study conducted by McKinsey & Company found that companies in the top quartile for gender diversity on executive teams are 25% more likely to experience above-average profitability compared to those in the bottom quartile. This correlation between gender diversity and financial performance suggests that women leaders bring unique perspectives that enhance problem-solving and creativity, driving better business outcomes.

Women-led companies often have a more comprehensive understanding of their customer base, particularly as women control a significant portion of consumer spending. Research indicates that women influence more than 70% of all consumer purchasing decisions. Female leaders can leverage this insight to create products and marketing strategies that resonate with a broader audience, thus expanding market reach.

It is also important to recognize that the advantages of diverse leadership extend beyond gender and should be looked at more widely and with an intersectional lens to gain truly gain benefit from a diversity angle. There are various studies that have shown that other groups – such as racial and ethnic minorities, LGBTQ+ individuals, and people with disabilities – also contribute significantly to organizational success, profitability and innovation.

Organizations with racially and ethnically diverse leadership teams often see improved performance and innovation. According to a study by McKinsey & Company, companies in the top quartile for ethnic diversity on executive teams are 36% more likely to achieve above-average profitability compared to those in the bottom quartile.

Companies that embrace LGBTQ+ diversity also experience positive business outcomes. Research indicates that organizations that prioritize LGBTQ+ inclusion not only attract a broader customer base but also benefit from enhanced employee satisfaction and retention rates. Companies known for inclusive policies, that have integrated LGBTQ+ advocacy into their corporate ethos, have found that they have stronger brand loyalty and a diverse workforce that drives innovation. A company's commitment to LGBTQ+ rights can attract a dedicated customer base, supporting the business case for inclusivity.

Including people with disabilities in the workforce can also lead to improved performance and innovation by fostering diverse perspectives, enhancing problem-solving capabilities and creating a more adaptable and inclusive workplace culture. A study by

Accenture found that companies that are more inclusive of individuals with disabilities achieve 28% higher revenue and double the net income compared to their peers. This is likely due to the fact that inclusive companies benefit from a wider talent pool, greater employee engagement and stronger brand reputation.

Employees with disabilities often bring unique problem-solving skills, resilience and adaptability – qualities that can drive innovation and improve business outcomes. Their experiences navigating challenges can lead to the development of more creative solutions that benefit both internal processes and customer interactions. Additionally, when companies invest in accessibility and inclusion, they often discover improvements that benefit all employees, such as more flexible work arrangements and the use of assistive technologies that enhance overall productivity.

The evidence is clear: diversity in leadership, whether through gender, race, sexual orientation or disability status or through an intersectional lens – drives better business performance and innovation. Organizations that prioritize inclusivity can tap into a wider range of perspectives, ultimately leading to enhanced creativity, improved problem-solving and greater market relevance. By cultivating an environment where diverse voices are heard and valued, companies position themselves for long-term success and a competitive edge in the marketplace.

BRAND ACTIVISM

Brand activism refers to the commitment of companies to advocate for social change and address societal issues through their business practices and marketing efforts. For millennials, this commitment is not just a preference but an expectation. Research shows that this demographic is more inclined to support brands that align with their values and demonstrate social responsibility. In an era where social media amplifies voices and movements, brands that remain silent on critical issues risk alienating potential customers. A study from *Edelman* reinforces this notion, revealing that consumers are more likely to trust and purchase from brands that they perceive as socially responsible.

Recent market research studies by *Google and Ipsos* showed that 70% of Black millennials are more likely to purchase from brands that take a stand on race-related issues. This shows a clear and significant trend in consumer behaviour among younger demographics. This trend indicates that brand activism, particularly around social justice and racial equality, plays a crucial role in purchasing decisions for diverse groups as well as which products and services they are more likely to engage with.

The rise of social media has also contributed to this trend. Platforms like X formerly Twitter, Instagram and TikTok have become vital channels for consumers to express their expectations of brands and hold them accountable. Brands that fail to address racial issues publicly may face backlash and boycotts from consumers who demand authenticity and accountability. The viral nature of social media means that consumers can easily share their dissatisfaction, potentially damaging a brand's reputation and financial performance. This was evident with the backlash against companies that remained silent during the Black Lives Matter movement highlights the critical importance of taking a proactive stance on social justice.

Taking a stand on social justice related issues can enhance brand trust and loyalty. When brands speak out against injustice or support initiatives aimed at promoting Inclusion, they resonate more deeply with consumers, particularly millennials who are often more engaged in social issues. Brands that effectively communicate their support for inclusion initiatives can experience increased customer loyalty. This loyalty is often reflected in long-term purchasing behaviour, making it crucial for brands to align their messaging with actions that reflect genuine commitment rather than performative allyship.

However, brands must approach activism carefully. If not executed authentically, there is a risk of being perceived as opportunistic or insincere, which can lead to negative consumer sentiment. Brands need to conduct thorough research and engage with relevant communities to understand the issues and challenges they face. Additionally, they should measure the impact of their initiatives to ensure that they resonate with their target audiences.

As we look to the future, the demographics of consumers are also changing significantly, with Millennials and Generation Z leading the way in diversity. According to a report from *Gallup*, Millennials represent the most demographically diverse generation in the workforce, with 44.2% identifying as part of a minority race or ethnic group. Generation Z, which follows, is projected to be even more diverse. This shift presents both challenges and opportunities for businesses, emphasizing the importance of reflecting this diversity in products and services.

For these younger generations, seeing themselves represented in the brands they support is essential. They are more likely to connect with products that acknowledge and celebrate diversity, as this fosters a sense of belonging and authenticity. Brands that fail to do so risk alienating potential customers. A study by *Deloitte* highlights that 83% of Millennials believe it is important for brands to support D&I efforts. Consequently, companies that incorporate diverse perspectives into their offerings are likely to gain a competitive edge by resonating more deeply with this demographic.

Millennials and Generation Z are not just passive consumers; they are active participants in shaping market dynamics. They seek brands that align with their values, including social justice and equity. According to a report by *Accenture*, 63% of consumers prefer to purchase from companies that advocate for the issues they care about. This preference underscores the necessity for brands to actively promote diversity not only in their marketing but also in their product development processes.

Moreover, the demand for personalized and customizable products is on the rise among these generations. Brands that embrace inclusive design principles and allow consumers to tailor products to their unique preferences are better positioned to succeed. For instance, a global footwear brand has an initiative that empowers customers to design their own shoes, offering a personal touch that reflects individual identities. This level of engagement not only enhances customer satisfaction but also builds brand loyalty among diverse consumer groups.

It is important to note that this generational shift is not unique and together with advances in technology, over the years through various generations, new patterns around consumer behaviour and engagement have emerged. Many of us can recall the days of renting movies on DVD and VHS from a popular global chain. You'd pay a fee, enjoy your movie and return it within a set number of days, though more often than not, late fees were an inevitable part of the experience!

Today, that once-dominant rental service has completely disappeared from our towns and cities. Some argue that a lack of innovation or a missed opportunity to acquire what is now one of the biggest streaming services played a role in its downfall. While that may be true, another crucial factor was the failure to adapt to the changing needs and behaviours of future generations of customers.

This raises an important question for us today: Will we follow the same path, resisting change and fading into irrelevance? Or will we evolve to meet the ever-changing demands of our consumers and stay ahead of the curve?

As technology continues to advance and more and more people are now glued onto social media, we must not forget the role it plays in shaping consumer perceptions. Platforms like Instagram and TikTok have amplified the voices of a variety of influencers, making it crucial for brands to authentically represent D&I in their campaigns. Brands that engage with these platforms and showcase diverse narratives can capture the attention of younger audiences, fostering a deeper connection.

As Millennials and Generation Z become the dominant consumer groups, the expectation for diversity in products and services will only increase. Brands that prioritize inclusivity and actively reflect the diverse identities of their consumers will not only foster loyalty but also drive financial success. Understanding and embracing this demographic shift will be vital for organizations aiming to remain relevant and competitive in the ever-evolving marketplace.

IMPLEMENT INCLUSIVE DESIGN PRINCIPLES

Applying inclusive design principles aims to create products that are usable, accessible and enjoyable for the broadest possible range of people, no matter their backgrounds, abilities or circumstances. This approach involves incorporating the perspectives and needs of diverse users from the earliest stages of design. By proactively considering factors like physical abilities, cultural nuances, language preferences and socioeconomic barriers, inclusive design makes products more universally accessible and versatile. It also helps to prevent common design pitfalls that may unintentionally exclude certain groups.

Incorporating inclusive design goes beyond simply meeting accessibility standards; it also emphasizes adaptability, empathy and flexibility in product use. For instance, designing customizable user settings in software allows people to adjust text size, contrast and language, which can improve usability for users with visual impairments, non-native language speakers and even individuals with temporary limitations (e.g. those in bright sunlight). By creating adaptable features, designers address a range of use cases and support individual autonomy, resulting in a product that is more widely appreciated and more likely to be used consistently.

It is essential to also remember that every diverse group is not the same and even though people might look the same, or have many or all similar diversity characteristics, they can still have different views or opinions on products and services. That is why it is important to regularly engage as many diverse perspectives in research as possible, even from the same groups. Through this wider and continuous engagement, companies gain insights that ensure products and services genuinely meet consumer needs and avoid cultural missteps.

Accessible design goes beyond compliance; it makes products more versatile, easier to use and accessible to diverse groups, ultimately broadening a company's market reach and enhancing its reputation for social responsibility. When accessibility is integrated from the beginning, it yields products that are more intuitive and efficient, not only for individuals with disabilities but often for all users, creating a better user experience and encouraging brand loyalty.

The addition of accessibility features, such as information on wheelchair-accessible routes and entrances, has made navigation apps invaluable for people with mobility limitations, while also benefiting users pushing strollers or carrying luggage. These accessibility-focused updates increase usability for diverse audiences and exemplify a commitment to serving a broader range of needs.

LOCALIZE AND CULTURALLY ADAPT PRODUCTS

It is important for companies who offer products and services in multiple regions, to ensure they are culturally adapted to meet the needs and preferences of local audiences. This includes translating content into different languages, adapting imagery and symbols to resonate with different cultures, and considering local customs and norms in the product design. Cultural sensitivity helps to avoid alienating or offending users in different markets.

Adapting products and services to local cultures is a vital strategy for businesses aiming to thrive in diverse markets. This process, often referred to as localization, goes beyond mere translation of text; it encompasses a thorough understanding of the cultural, social and economic contexts of the target audience. Companies must research local customs, consumer behaviours and societal values to ensure their offerings resonate effectively with different populations.

One of the critical aspects of localization is language. Effective communication in the local dialect is essential, requiring not just direct translation but an understanding of cultural nuances and idiomatic expressions. Many brands have successfully localized their marketing strategies by using language that aligns with local culture, which helps them connect more deeply with consumers. Additionally, product design may need to be modified to cater to local preferences. A popular modular construction Toy company has introduced themed sets that celebrate local history and landmarks, creating a stronger connection with their audience.

Compliance with local customs and regulations is also a necessary consideration in the localization process. Businesses must ensure their products adhere to local safety standards, laws and cultural expectations. For example, many food and beverage companies tailor their offerings to comply with dietary restrictions and health regulations specific to different regions and also adapt their food to meet religious needs like Halal food in the Middle East and no Beef products in India.

Culture can also differ from country to country and even though something might be legally acceptable it is important to note that it might not be culturally appropriate, for example an ad showing a couple kissing, this would be culturally acceptable in many western countries but could be deemed culturally inappropriate in other markets. Therefore, going beyond just legal requirements and deepening your understanding of local cultural differences and preferences is crucial to achieve success for your product or service.

Building partnerships with local entities can greatly enhance a company's understanding of the market. Collaborations with local influencers or businesses can provide invaluable insights that drive more culturally relevant marketing and product strategies. For instance, some hospitality platforms leverage local expertise to curate authentic travel experiences that align with community values, enhancing customer trust and satisfaction.

Ongoing engagement and feedback from local consumers are crucial. Brands must adapt and refine their offerings based on real user experiences and preferences. Some music streaming platforms exemplify this by continuously curating playlists that reflect regional trends and user input, ensuring they remain relevant across diverse markets and audiences.

By implementing these strategies, businesses can create products that not only meet local demands but also foster inclusivity and customer loyalty. In today's interconnected marketplace, embracing cultural diversity through thoughtful localization can provide companies with a significant competitive edge, driving both market success and brand reputation.

USE INCLUSIVE LANGUAGE AND IMAGERY

Language has a profound impact on how users relate to a product. Choosing inclusive language involves using terms that are respectful and do not exclude or marginalize individuals. This includes adopting gender-neutral language and avoiding jargon that may alienate specific groups. Research from the *American Psychological Association* supports the notion that using inclusive language minimizes bias and fosters a more welcoming environment, particularly in user instructions and marketing materials.

When crafting messages, it is essential to understand the cultural nuances of language. It is also important to understand that many words when translated into different languages can mean different things, and therefore a word that means something different in one language when translated can end up meaning something completely different.

Visual elements play a significant role in communicating inclusivity. Brands should utilize images that represent a broad spectrum of demographics, including different races, ages, body types and abilities. For example, a well-known personal care brand successfully demonstrated that campaigns featuring diverse representations of beauty, including women of different sizes, lead to higher engagement and improved brand perception. Similarly, other major beauty brands have made significant strides in embracing visual diversity in their marketing, with a focus on promoting beauty for all. Their campaigns often feature models of different ethnicities, skin tones and ages.

To effectively gauge the inclusivity of language and imagery, it's vital to involve a diverse group of users during the design process. Conducting user testing with participants from various backgrounds can help identify biases or exclusions in the design. For example, some leading tech companies incorporate diverse focus groups to assess their products, ensuring that the end result is inclusive and meets a wide range of user needs. Engaging diverse users for feedback in product design and services is essential for ensuring that offerings are inclusive and cater to a broad audience.

COMMITMENT TO ONGOING EDUCATION

Companies should stay updated on diversity trends and promote continuous learning among team members regarding inclusive practices. This commitment to education fosters a culture that prioritizes inclusivity in design processes as well as ensuring that companies are adapting to the changing needs of its customers. Sometimes what might have been acceptable in the past changes and is now not acceptable. This can be the result of social justice, a particular incident or just generational change on what it deems to be acceptable and not acceptable.

A well-known clothing brand made a commitment to stop sexualizing models in its advertising, despite previously being known for its controversial and provocative campaigns in the early 2000s. This shift was driven by changing consumer expectations, evolving societal views on the portrayal of models, and broader trends in the fashion industry regarding what was considered acceptable. The brand worked to reposition itself by focusing on inclusivity, body positivity and a more respectful approach to advertising, which ultimately led to more positive engagement with its customers.

Organizations should invest in regular training sessions and workshops focused on inclusive design principles. These can be conducted by external experts or internal teams and can cover a range of topics, including conscious inclusion, global cultural competency and accessibility standards. For example, the Design Thinking for Diversity workshop offered by IDEO teaches teams how to create inclusive products by integrating diverse perspectives from the start of the design process. Regular training helps keep Inclusion of all groups, top-of-mind and allows team members to stay updated on best practices.

Staying informed through literature is crucial. Organizations should encourage teams to read books, articles and research papers on inclusive design. Key texts include 'Designing for Diversity' by Tenny Pinheiro and 'The Inclusive Design Toolkit' by the University of Cambridge. Journals such as the *Journal of Usability Studies* and the *International Journal of Human-Computer Interaction* frequently publish research on inclusive practices and innovations.

ADDRESS BIAS IN AI AND ALGORITHMS

If your products or services use AI or algorithms, ensure that these systems are designed to minimize bias and promote equity. This includes auditing algorithms for potential biases, training AI models on diverse data sets, and involving diverse teams in the development and testing of AI-driven products. Transparent and accountable AI practices can prevent the unintentional reinforcement of societal biases.

The first step in combating bias is to ensure that the data used for training AI models is diverse and representative. This means actively collecting data that includes a wide array of demographics such as race, gender, age and socioeconomic background. Many companies have worked on diversifying their datasets to improve the performance of facial recognition technologies and reduce inherent biases. Implementing a Data Ethics Framework can guide organizations in evaluating their data for fairness and representation which can prevent user experiences that contain biases.

To effectively identify bias, organizations should perform comprehensive audits of their AI algorithms. Regular impact assessments can help understand how these systems affect different demographic groups. *The Algorithmic Justice League* has developed bias detection tools to scrutinize algorithms, ensuring that they do not reinforce stereotypes or inequalities. Conducting these assessments both before and after deployment helps maintain accountability.

Transparency in AI algorithms is crucial for accountability and trust. By making the processes behind algorithms clear, organizations can allow stakeholders to understand how decisions are made. The Partnership on AI emphasizes the need for organizations to document their algorithmic processes, including data sources and decision-making frameworks. This practice fosters trust and enables external evaluations of potential biases.

Integrating inclusive design principles during the development phase can enhance the relevance and fairness of AI systems. This means assembling diverse teams and involving representatives from communities affected by the technology in the design process. Some leading tech companies actively practice inclusive design by incorporating user feedback from various demographics, resulting in products that better serve all users. For example, voice-activated assistants are continuously improved to accommodate diverse accents, languages and dialects, ensuring that people from various backgrounds can interact with the technology more effectively.

Bias is not static and can change over time. Therefore, organizations must establish mechanisms for continuous learning, enabling AI systems to evolve with new information and changing societal norms. This might include updating models with new data or utilizing feedback loops for users to report issues.

Creating a framework for ethical AI governance helps ensure ongoing commitment to addressing bias. Organizations can form dedicated teams focused on ethical practices, ensuring compliance with Inclusion principles throughout the AI lifecycle. Guidelines from the *IEEE Global Initiative on Ethics of Autonomous and Intelligent Systems* offer comprehensive recommendations for the ethical design and deployment of AI technologies.

By integrating these strategies, organizations can strive to create AI systems that are not only equitable but also aligned with the diverse needs of users. This commitment to addressing bias enhances product integrity and fosters trust in technology which with the continued advancement of AI will be an important element to get right in order to continue to build products, services and user experiences that are free from bias and stereotypes.

CREATE FLEXIBLE AND CUSTOMIZABLE SOLUTIONS

Design products and services that can be easily customized to meet the diverse needs of different users. Providing options for users to personalize their experience, such as adjustable settings or customizable features, can help accommodate a wide range of preferences and requirements. Flexibility in product design allows users to tailor the experience to their unique needs.

Creating products with adjustable settings empowers users to tailor their experiences to fit their individual needs. For example, many modern devices offer a range of accessibility features, such as screen readers for visually impaired users, adjustable text sizes and colour filters for those with colour blindness. By providing these options, companies not only enhance accessibility but also allow users to interact with their devices in ways that best suit their personal preferences. This approach demonstrates how customizable features can foster a sense of ownership and comfort for diverse user groups.

Modular design allows users to select components that best meet their specific needs. For example, certain furniture systems are designed for easy assembly and customization, enabling customers to choose different sizes, colours and configurations to create pieces that fit their space and style. This approach not only addresses varied aesthetic preferences but also accommodates different functional requirements, such as storage needs or space limitations. Such flexibility encourages creativity and personal expression while making products more inclusive.

Leveraging data analytics and artificial intelligence can enhance customization. For example, a major streaming company uses algorithms to analyze viewing habits and provide personalized recommendations for shows and movies. This approach caters to diverse tastes and interests, ensuring that content feels relevant to each user. By enabling users to create a personalized viewing experience, many streaming services demonstrate how data-driven insights and customization can lead to increased engagement and satisfaction amongst consumers.

Products can also be customized to reflect diverse cultural backgrounds and preferences. For instance, many language-learning apps now allow users to choose their preferred dialect and incorporates culturally relevant content into its courses. This ensures that learners engage with materials that resonate with their cultural context, enhancing both relatability and effectiveness in language acquisition. Such considerations not only improve learning outcomes but also demonstrate respect for cultural diversity.

Incorporating customizable options in product and service design is not merely about enhancing usability; it is about fostering inclusivity and engagement across diverse user groups. By prioritizing user-centric customization, companies can create experiences that resonate with individual preferences and requirements, ultimately leading to greater satisfaction and loyalty.

MEASURE AND ITERATE ON INCLUSION IMPACT

Regularly assessing the impact of your products and services on diverse user groups by collecting and analyzing data related to Inclusion outcomes helps ensure your products and services are fit for purpose. This can include user satisfaction surveys, accessibility audits and impact assessments focused on equity. Use this data to identify areas for improvement and iterate on your designs to better meet the needs of all users. Continuous improvement is key to ensuring that Inclusion remains a central consideration in your offerings.

A comprehensive approach involves various quantitative and qualitative methods that evaluate user experiences, product accessibility and overall satisfaction among different demographic groups. Here are some effective strategies for assessing the impact of inclusion in product design and service delivery.

Conducting regular user satisfaction surveys can provide valuable insights into how different user groups perceive inclusivity in products and services. These surveys can be designed to include specific questions regarding accessibility features, usability for diverse populations and overall satisfaction levels. These audits can be conducted using both automated tools and human testing to ensure a comprehensive assessment. For instance, a large software developer conducts accessibility checks on their software, ensuring that features like screen readers and text-to-speech are effective for users with visual impairments.

Engaging with communities directly can provide invaluable feedback. This can involve attending community events, partnering with local organizations, or holding workshops where users can interact with prototypes and share their thoughts. For instance, a popular hospitality platform collaborates with local hosts to understand their unique needs and experiences, which helps the company refine its offerings to better serve diverse markets. By engaging directly with local hosts, the platform is also able to implement localized safety measures, policies and pricing strategies. Hosts may provide valuable insights into local laws, customs or practices that the company might not have considered otherwise. This helps mitigate risks and ensures the platform's accessibility and inclusivity while respecting the cultural context of each market.

Creating an ongoing feedback loop with users allows for continuous improvement to your products and services. After implementing changes based on initial feedback, companies should return to users to assess the effectiveness of those changes as well as insights from other users on if the changes impacted their user experiences. This iterative process was employed by a music streaming service, which frequently adjusts its features based on user feedback, ensuring that its platform remains relevant and user-friendly as well as ensuring they adjust their features regularly to meet the changing needs of its customers.

Social media platforms and online communities provide an accessible avenue for gathering feedback from diverse users. Brands can engage in conversations, solicit opinions and monitor discussions to gauge public sentiment about their products. For example, a well-known coffee chain has used social media as a tool to connect with customers and get real-time feedback on products. One of the best examples of this is their #WhatsYourName campaign, which aimed to engage LGBTQIA+ customers. The company actively uses social media platforms to promote new products and ask for feedback.

Their social media channels also allow customers to express their opinions about specific items, whether they love or dislike a particular drink or if they think the company could improve certain aspects of their service. The brand even has a dedicated app where customers can rate their experiences, which the company uses to make quick adjustments to both service and product offerings.

Using Inclusion analytics can help organizations assess how well their products and services cater to varied user groups. This involves collecting demographic data about users and analyzing usage patterns across different segments. By leveraging these insights companies can identify gaps in their offerings and make data-driven decisions to enhance inclusion.

Conducting impact assessments that focus specifically on equity can help organizations evaluate how their products affect different user groups. For example, Many Police forces in the UK utilize Community Impact Assessments before any major event or police activity to analyze the implications on communities, ensuring that any potential adverse effects are identified and addressed in advance. Such assessments can help organizations in identifying potential risks early own and allow organizations to adapt and plan for potential risks at an early stage.

Organizations should establish metrics for continuous improvement in inclusion outcomes. For example, tracking changes in user satisfaction over time can provide insights into whether efforts to enhance inclusion are effective. By systematically evaluating these aspects, organizations can gain a clearer understanding of how well they are meeting the needs of diverse user groups and make informed decisions to enhance inclusivity in their offerings.

By embedding these strategies into your product and service development processes, you can create offerings that are not only inclusive and equitable but also more innovative and impactful, resonating with a broader and more diverse customer base.

6

CREATING MEANINGFUL INCLUSION PROGRAMMES AND INITIATIVES

Meaningful inclusion initiatives are not merely feel-good activities; they should align with the organization's overall business strategy. By embedding inclusion into the core operations and objectives of the business, companies can drive innovation, improve employee satisfaction and enhance financial performance. Random acts of diversity often result in short-lived impacts. In contrast, meaningful programmes focus on long-term systemic change. This involves analyzing existing barriers to inclusion, creating accountability measures and regularly assessing the effectiveness of initiatives. Successful diversity programmes must be sustained and embedded in the organizational culture to yield significant benefits. Random acts of diversity may create temporary positive sentiments but fail to address underlying issues that perpetuate exclusion.

Organizations that engage in genuine inclusion efforts foster trust among all employees and stakeholders. When employees see that their company is committed to meaningful change, they are more likely to feel valued and included. Conversely, superficial initiatives can lead to scepticism and disengagement. Authenticity is crucial for building lasting relationships with employees and customers alike. This commitment not only benefits marginalized groups but enriches the entire organizational culture and drives overall success.

Often many organizations hold back on the development of programmes and initiatives because they are not sure if it is a 100% right. The truth is no one has the perfect solution and if someone did you would not be here reading this, we would have solved for inclusion years ago and had a textbook formula that we could apply across all organizations. What we must get accustomed to is failure in our inclusion efforts. Many programmes and initiatives fail and failure is not bad, it shows you tried, what is important is that you learn from that failure and try again but this time building in the lessons learnt.

ASSESS THE CURRENT STATE OF INCLUSION

In order to understand your current state of inclusion, it is important to conduct a thorough assessment of the organization's current inclusion landscape. This includes collecting demographic data, analyzing employee surveys and reviewing hiring and retention statistics. It is essential to start by understanding not only who comprises your organization, but also the environment they are working within. This can be broken down into several key steps:

1. Collect Demographic Data

Begin by gathering comprehensive data on employee demographics across various levels of the organization. These data typically include race, gender, age, disability status, sexual orientation (if voluntarily provided) and other identifiers that highlight representation gaps. Demographic data should be collected while ensuring confidentiality and informed consent to build trust and accuracy in responses.

2. Analyze Employee Surveys and Feedback

Implement regular, anonymous employee surveys to gauge feelings around inclusion, belonging and equity within the workplace. These surveys can assess the organizational culture, identify potential bias and gather insights into employees' experiences of inclusivity. Surveys should include open-ended questions to capture nuanced feedback and give employees the opportunity to share their thoughts openly.

3. Review Hiring, Promotion and Retention Metrics

Analyze hiring data to understand diversity in recruitment practices, identifying any bottlenecks in attracting diverse talent. Examining promotion and retention rates among diverse groups provides insight into career advancement and retention gaps. For example, lower promotion rates among certain groups may indicate potential biases in performance evaluations or developmental opportunities, while higher turnover rates could suggest a lack of support or inclusive practices.

4. Examine Pay Equity and Benefits

Conduct a pay equity analysis to identify disparities across demographic groups. Compensation and benefits should align with market standards and offer flexibility to meet diverse needs, such as parental leave and mental health support, ensuring they contribute to equitable treatment.

5. Evaluate Training and Development Programmes

Assess current training programmes related to inclusion, including implicit bias and inclusive leadership. Evaluate whether these programmes are effective in equipping employees with the skills they need to foster an inclusive workplace and where gaps may exist. This can also involve reviewing participation data and effectiveness metrics to refine training efforts continuously.

6. Benchmark Against Industry Standards

Comparing the organization's diversity data with industry standards or national benchmarks provides additional context. This helps in setting realistic goals and identifying where the organization stands relative to competitors and sector-wide inclusion progress.

7. Conduct Focus Groups or Listening Sessions

Supplement quantitative data with qualitative insights by organizing focus groups with employees from underrepresented groups. This approach can uncover experiences and perspectives that might not emerge through surveys, giving a clearer picture of day-to-day inclusivity challenges.

By combining these methods, organizations can create a complete view of their inclusion landscape and pinpoint specific areas needing improvement, from recruitment and onboarding to career advancement and overall workplace culture. The data gathered serves as a baseline for setting measurable inclusion objectives, tracking progress over time, and ensuring ongoing accountability for sustainable change through establishing a clear baseline of where the organization stands in terms of diversity and inclusion.

SET CLEAR OBJECTIVES

Setting inclusion objectives can significantly drive an organization towards a more inclusive and equitable environment, creating clear paths for improvement and demonstrating a tangible commitment to change. When inclusion objectives are established, they allow an organization to track its progress effectively and hold leaders accountable, ensuring that inclusion remains a central focus rather than a vague aspiration.

These objectives also play a crucial role in enhancing employee engagement and fostering trust, especially among underrepresented groups. For job candidates, inclusion objectives often make an organization more appealing as they signal that inclusion is taken seriously, strengthening the brand as an employer of choice.

However, setting inclusion objectives does come with challenges and potential risks. One concern is the possibility of tokenism, where the drive to meet specific diversity metrics can lead to superficial changes rather than meaningful cultural shifts. This can result in an environment where diversity numbers appear favourable on the surface, but the lived experiences of employees tell a different

story. There is also the risk of internal resistance and external backlash, as some may view inclusion objectives, especially those tied to representation, as unfair or rigid, sparking division within teams if not communicated carefully.

Furthermore, accurately measuring inclusion progress is inherently complex; metrics around qualitative aspects like belonging or inclusion can be difficult to standardize and quantify, yet are critical to capturing the true impact of the efforts.

Another challenge with inclusion objectives is that a strong focus on numbers might oversimplify inclusion, overlooking the need for cultural transformation that supports inclusion beyond representation metrics. Increasing diversity in hiring is only one part of the equation; fostering an environment that supports retention and advancement for all, is equally essential for sustainable progress. Addressing these risks involves ensuring that inclusion objectives are part of a broader, comprehensive inclusion strategy, with input from different voices to ensure these goals are both realistic and meaningful.

Including qualitative assessments, regularly revisiting and adjusting objectives, and fostering open communication about inclusion objectives are all strategies that can help organizations avoid pitfalls, build sustainable cultural change and create an environment where inclusion is embedded in every aspect of the organization.

Beyond traditional diversity representation metrics, organizations can focus on a broader range of employee experience and engagement goals to build a well-rounded inclusion approach. This includes setting goals to improve scores in employee surveys, particularly around feelings of respect, psychological safety and belonging. Tracking retention rates and advancement opportunities for different groups can also help identify and close gaps, ensuring all employees have equal access to growth opportunities and leadership roles. Development opportunities for diverse employees are another focus, with goals to increase participation rates in training and leadership programmes.

Exit interviews can also provide valuable feedback on inclusion experiences, helping to uncover and address any systemic challenges faced by different groups. Diverse team collaboration is another area for improvement, with objectives to ensure a mix of backgrounds in project teams and all leaders receiving feedback on inclusivity. Engagement with events, such as employee resource groups (ERGs) and celebratory days, can also be tracked for participation and satisfaction to promote a sense of belonging across the organization.

Setting inclusion objectives can be approached in various ways, and it's not always necessary to focus solely on representation percentages. Depending on the organization's priorities and capacity for data collection and goal monitoring, inclusion objectives can be centred around qualitative measures, such as creating an inclusive culture, fostering diversity of thought, or implementing specific policies that promote equality in the workplace. The approach chosen should align with the company's values, its overall inclusion strategy, and the long-term goals it hopes to achieve regarding inclusion and equity.

When organizations choose to use representation metrics, the first critical step is defining the baseline. This involves gathering comprehensive data on current workforce demographics across all levels, functions and locations. By collecting this data, organizations gain valuable insights into the diversity of their existing workforce. This includes not just basic demographic information like gender, race, ethnicity and age, but also deeper factors like disability status, LGBTQ+ representation and socio-economic background, depending on the data being tracked.

This analysis helps reveal areas where certain groups are underrepresented or absent, such as in senior leadership roles, specific departments or geographic regions. For example, if the data shows that women or racial minorities are underrepresented in technical or executive positions, it highlights areas for improvement and sets a foundation for setting specific objectives.

After identifying these gaps, organizations can then develop initiatives aimed at addressing the disparities. These objectives might include focused recruitment efforts, leadership development programmes, mentorship opportunities or improving retention through inclusive practices. The goal is to move beyond simply filling quotas and ensure that diverse voices and perspectives are integrated and valued throughout all levels of the organization.

Tracking the involvement of underrepresented groups in professional development initiatives is another approach, supporting career progression and growth in a way that does not emphasize specific representation targets. Additionally, objectives might aim to increase participation in inclusion-related activities, such as training, ERG membership, or inclusion events.

Combining metrics with qualitative objectives offers a comprehensive view of inclusion progress. Organizations benefit from metrics that work in tandem with broader efforts to cultivate a supportive and inclusive culture for all. This combined approach aligns with the principles of SMART goal-setting – specific, measurable, actionable, relevant and time-bound – ensuring inclusion efforts are coherent with organizational objectives and adaptable as inclusion needs evolve. Whether relying on metrics data or qualitative measures, both approaches prioritize ongoing growth and accountability in the pursuit of inclusion progress.

To create a roadmap that aligns inclusion with organizational priorities, it's essential to begin by defining the company's key objectives, such as growth, customer satisfaction and innovation. Once these priorities are clear, it becomes easier to establish how inclusion can support them directly. For instance, if customer satisfaction is a major goal, having a diverse team in customer-facing roles can help address diverse customer needs effectively. For innovation, diversity in teams can lead to more creative problem-solving and product development.

Next, measurable objectives should be set, linking directly to business objectives. These objectives might include increasing the representation of underrepresented groups or improving employee perceptions of inclusivity. These objectives should be actionable, with a detailed implementation plan that includes milestones, timelines and checkpoints for regular review.

Creating internal partnerships and accountability mechanisms ensures that every department plays a role in inclusion. Leaders across departments can act as inclusion champions, linking inclusion initiatives with specific business functions, like inclusive hiring practices in HR or inclusive design principles in product development. Building a supportive culture is also crucial for retention and engagement, so initiatives like leadership training, ERGs and open feedback channels can help nurture an environment where everyone feels valued.

Ongoing measurement and analysis of inclusion progress, including tools like employee surveys and diversity dashboards, help track the impact of inclusion on broader organizational priorities. Continuous monitoring means inclusion strategies can be adjusted in response to emerging challenges and evolving company goals. This data-driven approach ensures that inclusion efforts remain relevant and effective.

Transparency around progress is also important. Regular updates build trust and accountability, while celebrating milestones reinforces commitment to inclusion as a strategic priority. Finally, as the company grows and priorities evolve, the inclusion strategy must remain flexible to align with new goals, which may include reaching new markets or expanding customer diversity. This flexibility ensures inclusion remains a valuable part of the organization's long-term strategy, contributing to a more inclusive, resilient and innovative business.

ENGAGE LEADERSHIP AND STAKEHOLDERS

Engaging leadership and stakeholders when developing inclusion programmes and initiatives is critical for ensuring that inclusion is integrated into an organization's culture and strategic goals. Successful inclusion programmes are often those that have the full backing of senior leadership, as their involvement signals a commitment to creating a more inclusive environment. Here's a comprehensive approach for engaging leadership and stakeholders in inclusion initiatives:

Before engaging leadership, it's essential to demonstrate the clear business value of inclusion. Research shows that diverse teams drive innovation, improve decision-making and lead to better financial outcomes. For example, *McKinsey's report 'Diversity Wins'* found that companies in the top quartile for ethnic diversity are 36% more likely to have above-average profitability. Presenting such data can help leaders understand the ROI of inclusion efforts. Additionally, aligning inclusion objectives with organizational priorities like enhancing employee engagement, improving customer experiences or increasing market share can make the case even more compelling.

Leaders need to understand that inclusion is not just a set of programmes or HR initiatives; it is a strategic priority that affects the bottom line. To engage leaders, explain how inclusion initiatives can align with and support the company's overarching goals, such as customer satisfaction, market growth and retention of top talent.

To gain buy-in from key stakeholders, involve them from the start. This includes engaging department heads, HR, ERGs and other influential figures within the organization. By gathering input and feedback from stakeholders, you can ensure that inclusion programmes reflect the diverse needs of the entire organization. For instance, when developing inclusion strategies, it's helpful to host listening sessions or workshops where employees can provide feedback on what they believe the company needs in terms of diversity and inclusion. This fosters a sense of ownership and investment from the leadership and key stakeholders.

Leaders are more likely to invest in inclusion initiatives when they understand their accountability. Setting specific, measurable objectives – such as improving representation, reducing turnover rates for groups or increasing employee satisfaction scores related to inclusion, helps demonstrate tangible outcomes. For inclusion to be truly effective, leaders and stakeholders must receive regular updates on progress, challenges and successes. Establishing clear communication channels ensures that everyone is aligned with the inclusion objectives. This could include quarterly or annual reports, town halls or inclusion updates during leadership meetings.

Leadership should model the behaviours they expect from their teams. When senior leaders publicly demonstrate their commitment to inclusion through their actions and decisions – such as prioritizing inclusive hiring practices, supporting ERGs, or addressing inequities within the organization – it sets the tone for the rest of the company. Leaders who make inclusion a visible priority are far more likely to inspire similar behaviours across the organization.

Supporting inclusion initiatives requires appropriate resources, including funding, time and personnel. Engaging leadership means ensuring they understand the level of investment required for success. For instance, setting up a dedicated inclusion office with a team that can work cross-functionally with departments like HR, marketing and product design ensures that inclusion efforts are integrated into the entire organizational fabric. Leaders should be encouraged to support these initiatives through financial investment and operational resources.

Effective inclusion programmes often require input from all levels of the organization. Engaging various departments and stakeholders like HR, marketing, communications, finance and operations, ensures that inclusion principles are woven into every aspect of the organization's work. This approach allows for holistic and sustainable inclusion strategies that can be seamlessly integrated into business processes.

Engaging leadership and stakeholders in inclusion programmes involves making a compelling business case, aligning inclusion with strategic priorities, involving key stakeholders early in the process, ensuring clear accountability, providing education and maintaining transparency. By fostering strong leadership commitment and involving various levels of the organization, companies can create more sustainable, effective inclusion initiatives that drive both social and business outcomes.

DEVELOP TARGETED PROGRAMMES

Designing and implementing inclusion programmes that specifically address the unique needs of different groups in the workplace is crucial to fostering an inclusive and supportive environment. These programmes should be intentional, targeted and aligned with organizational goals to ensure that all employees, particularly those from marginalized communities, have the opportunity to thrive. Here are some key inclusion programmes with examples of how companies can implement them effectively:

Mentorship programmes that connect employees from underrepresented groups with senior leaders can help bridge the gap in career advancement opportunities. These programmes offer guidance, career advice and networking opportunities that may otherwise be inaccessible to marginalized groups. Establishing such mentorship initiatives ensures that underrepresented employees receive the support they need to succeed, increasing the likelihood of their promotion into leadership roles.

Inclusive hiring practices, such as blind recruitment, aim to reduce biases in the hiring process, ensuring candidates from all backgrounds are considered fairly. By anonymizing resumes or using software that removes demographic information (such as gender, ethnicity or age), employers can focus on the skills and qualifications of candidates, rather than preconceived biases that may hinder the hiring process.

Cultural competency training is a key component of a comprehensive inclusion strategy. It helps employees understand the cultural norms, values and communication styles of different communities, fostering respect and collaboration. This training often includes learning about unconscious bias, microaggressions and ways to navigate cultural differences effectively in the workplace.

ERGs are voluntary, employee-led groups that foster a sense of community and support for individuals with common backgrounds or interests. These groups allow employees to come together, share experiences, provide mutual support and offer a collective voice in decision-making processes. ERGs are particularly valuable for employees from marginalized communities who may feel isolated in the workplace.

For inclusion programmes to be effective, they must also address career progression for underrepresented groups. This involves creating fair promotion processes that acknowledge the unique challenges marginalized employees face, as well as providing leadership development programmes. Ensuring equal opportunities for advancement helps reduce disparities in leadership representation.

Addressing bias in performance reviews is essential to ensure that employees receive fair and equitable evaluations. Many employees from underrepresented groups report being evaluated differently than their peers due to unconscious bias. Implementing structured and standardized performance reviews, with training to eliminate bias, ensures that all employees are assessed fairly.

These inclusion initiatives focus on providing equitable access to opportunities and resources for underrepresented groups. By fostering mentorship, implementing inclusive hiring practices, providing cultural competency training, supporting ERGs, creating equitable career advancement programmes and eliminating bias in performance evaluations, organizations can build a more inclusive and diverse workforce. Tailoring these programmes to meet the unique needs of different groups not only creates a fairer workplace but can also drive business performance, innovation and employee satisfaction.

ITERATE AND IMPROVE

Using insights from assessments and feedback to improve inclusion programmes is a strategic and essential approach to ensuring that these initiatives stay relevant, effective and aligned with organizational goals. Feedback collected from surveys, assessments and employee experiences can shed light on specific challenges, gaps and needs within the workforce. When these insights are applied thoughtfully, they provide a road map for adapting inclusion programmes to directly address areas that need growth or change. For example, if assessments reveal a lack of representation in certain departments, or if feedback highlights a need for improved inclusivity training, leadership can tailor programmes to target these issues specifically.

Refining inclusion programmes based on feedback involves both immediate actions and long-term adjustments. In the short term, insights might prompt the creation of targeted workshops, such as training sessions focused on unconscious bias or cultural competency. For instance, if feedback indicates that team members feel marginalized in decision-making, the organization might implement a mentorship programme aimed at empowering underrepresented employees. Additionally, regular pulse surveys can gauge the ongoing impact of these adjustments, helping leadership understand if new interventions are positively influencing the company culture and employees' sense of belonging.

On a larger scale, consistent assessment data can help leaders identify systemic issues and guide the strategic evolution of inclusion efforts. For example, feedback highlighting barriers to career progression for underrepresented groups can lead to a complete re-evaluation of promotion and performance review processes. By integrating insights from assessments into an ongoing improvement loop, companies can establish inclusion programmes that remain responsive to the workforce's needs. This adaptive approach signals to employees that their voices matter and that the organization is committed to creating a more inclusive, equitable environment.

Ultimately, using assessment-driven insights to shape inclusion programmes fosters a culture of continuous improvement. This approach not only strengthens inclusion efforts but also builds credibility and trust among employees, demonstrating that the organization is committed to meaningful and responsive change rather than surface-level initiatives.

FAIL FAST AND TRY AGAIN

Embracing a 'fail fast, learn, and try again' philosophy in inclusion work is especially essential given the complexity and sensitivity surrounding diversity, and inclusion. Unlike some traditional business processes that operate within predictable frameworks, inclusion initiatives involve deeply human issues that are both highly personal and vary widely across demographics and experiences. Implementing inclusion programmes, therefore, requires flexibility, humility and an acceptance that some approaches will inevitably fall short or need refinement. This approach ensures that inclusion initiatives are not only responsive but also more authentic in meeting the needs of an increasingly diverse workforce and consumer base.

When a company commits to this iterative approach, it creates a culture that values learning from setbacks. For example, a tech company might introduce an algorithmic screening tool to help reduce bias in hiring but later discover that the tool inadvertently perpetuates some existing biases due to flawed training data. Rather than persisting with a tool that isn't delivering on inclusion goals, the company can take this setback as a prompt to re-evaluate its process, refine the tool, or consider alternatives that involve more human oversight. This course correction, far from being a failure, is a sign of the organization's commitment to meaningful and effective inclusion.

Another key advantage of this approach is that it models an inclusive mindset in its very methodology. By openly acknowledging areas where programmes can improve, organizations demonstrate vulnerability and openness – qualities that invite honest feedback from employees, stakeholders and community members. For instance, by engaging with ERGs or holding open feedback sessions, companies can gather insights that may reveal underlying challenges that would otherwise go unnoticed. This not only improves programme effectiveness but also deepens trust within the workforce, as employees feel heard and valued.

'Fail fast, learn, and try again' is also practical for measuring inclusion programme success, which is inherently long-term. Unlike other corporate goals that may show clear results in financial quarters, inclusion progress is often gradual and non-linear. Programmes that allow for quick learning cycles, therefore, build momentum as they go, improving incrementally based on real-world insights. In essence, this approach transforms inclusion from a static set of goals into a dynamic, evolving process, one that adapts to the changing needs and voices of employees

This iterative, learning-focused approach turns inclusion work into a living framework, one that adapts to the complexities of changing workforce demographics, diverse employee needs and evolving societal expectations.

7

MEASURING AND TRACKING INCLUSION IMPACT AND PROGRESS

In today's rapidly evolving workplace, inclusion has moved from a 'nice-to-have' to a critical component of organizational success. However, beyond setting goals and initiatives, companies need systematic ways to track and measure inclusion progress to ensure they are making real, sustainable changes. The ability to measure inclusion outcomes enables organizations to drive equitable practices, align with business objectives and foster accountability at all levels.

One of the primary reasons to measure inclusion progress is to foster accountability within the organization. Setting clear metrics and regularly reporting on them holds leaders and teams accountable for their commitments to diversity and inclusion. Research shows that organizations that track diversity metrics see a more significant increase in diversity and inclusion than those that do not. Inclusion reporting also builds trust with employees, stakeholders and consumers, signalling that the organization is serious about its commitments.

Regularly measuring inclusion allows organizations to identify gaps and challenges within their workforce and initiatives. For instance, if surveys reveal low engagement scores among a particular group, companies can investigate the root causes and take targeted action. Organizations that actively measure inclusion progress are better equipped to implement meaningful changes as well as make informed decisions that drive effective interventions.

Tracking inclusion progress helps organizations to create a culture of continuous improvement. By regularly assessing the impact of inclusion initiatives, businesses can learn what works and what doesn't, allowing for iterative refinements. Organizations that treat inclusion as a process rather than a one-time initiative are more successful in embedding these values into the fabric of their organization. This ongoing focus gives organizations the opportunities for growth and adaptation in response to changing societal norms and employee expectations.

Transparency around diversity metrics helps to build trust. When organizations share inclusion data, both internally and publicly, they signal their commitment to progress and allow stakeholders to hold them accountable. This transparency also empowers employees to feel more confident in the organization's commitment to inclusion, reinforcing employee engagement and retention. In a LinkedIn survey, nearly 47% of employees noted they would leave an organization that lacked a commitment to inclusion, underscoring the importance of transparency and accountability for long-term retention.

Organizations that measure inclusion progress often see improved employee engagement and retention. When employees know that their organization is committed to inclusion and that progress is being tracked, they are more likely to feel valued and included. Diverse teams are more engaged, and companies that prioritize inclusion tend to have higher retention rates. This results in better output and reduced turnover costs.

DEFINE CLEAR GOALS AND METRICS

The first step is setting specific, measurable inclusion goals. For example, if an organization wants to increase gender diversity in leadership, it could set a goal to reach a certain percentage of women in leadership roles within a specified timeframe where this would be legally possible. Clear goals help focus inclusion efforts and create a foundation for measuring success.

In my role at one of the UK's largest Newspapers, we faced a gender pay gap nearing 35% one of the widest in our industry.

Recognizing the need for dedicated action, we developed a series of initiatives to assess our progress and address the gap. A critical turning point was when the CEO set an ambitious goal of reaching a zero gender pay gap by 2025. Though the goal seemed nearly unattainable, the high standard served to catalyze our efforts.

With this clear target, we put rigorous measurement systems in place that allowed us to track incremental progress and directly link outcomes to the interventions we implemented. By setting such an ambitious benchmark, leaders felt a heightened accountability and often exceeded initial efforts to drive meaningful change. This approach fostered a culture of commitment to gender equity, with leaders consistently prioritizing pay equality in talent acquisition, promotions and compensation policies.

By aiming high and establishing clear metrics for success, we created a continuous feedback loop that motivated teams and empowered them to push boundaries, resulting in a marked reduction in the gender pay gap. This experience underscored how ambitious goal-setting, along with transparent progress tracking, can not only focus efforts but also elevate commitment to inclusion outcomes, even in the face of challenging statistics.

UNDERSTANDING REGIONAL VARIANCES

Another important point to consider when setting diversity objectives, is understanding the population makeup of different regions to ensure that goals are realistic and meaningful. For example, London has a highly diverse population with over 40% identifying as non-white, creating a talent pool that can support ambitious race and ethnicity targets in recruitment and representation efforts. However, a company office located in a more rural area or in a city like Newcastle, which has a significantly lower percentage of racially diverse residents, would need to adjust these goals accordingly. Applying identical goals across all offices might be ineffective or a organisation up for failure in areas with less racially diverse populations, as it doesn't reflect the actual talent pool available in those regions.

Tailoring goals to regional demographics allow companies to pursue diversity goals that are feasible and context-specific, enhancing inclusivity without setting unrealistic expectations. It ensures that the organization's inclusion strategy is rooted in the reality of each location, increasing the relevance of inclusion initiatives and promoting fair representation while fostering realistic growth in diversity across various sites. This region-sensitive approach can also increase the effectiveness of outreach, recruitment and retention, leading to stronger community relations and a more genuinely inclusive workplace.

COLLECT BASELINE DATA

Before launching or expanding inclusion programmes, organizations need to gather baseline data. By capturing the current state of diversity in the workforce, companies establish a starting point to compare future progress against. Baseline data may include demographic information, promotion rates and survey results on inclusion.

Collecting baseline data is foundational for setting realistic and measurable inclusion goals. Baseline data provides a snapshot of an organization's current diversity landscape, identifying representation, inclusion and equity gaps across demographics. It serves as a benchmark for tracking future inclusion efforts and gauging progress. Without this initial data, it would be difficult to determine areas for improvement, measure impact, or hold leadership accountable.

At one of the organisations I worked for, we recently ran a global campaign to try to collect demographic data globally from our employees in different regions, countries and cities. Some of the lessons we learnt when collecting demographic data across different countries, was that organizations must address legal, cultural and practical considerations to ensure compliance, cultural sensitivity and accurate representation. Privacy laws vary widely globally; for example, Europe's GDPR enforces strict guidelines on consent and handling of personal data, and some countries even prohibit gathering certain data types entirely. Cultural sensitivity is crucial as concepts of race, gender and other identity factors can differ significantly by region. This sensitivity extends to using appropriate and locally relevant terminology in surveys, which enhances clarity and promotes employee engagement.

It's also essential that participation is voluntary and anonymous, as employees must feel comfortable providing sensitive information without pressure. Anonymizing responses builds trust and fosters honesty. Localization of survey language ensures that questions and terminology are accessible and culturally relevant. To make the data meaningful, we contextualized it through regional benchmarking, considered local demographic norms to set achievable, relevant goals.

We also ensured transparent communication about the purpose and use of data as well as sharing real examples of how we used diversity data in regions where we already had the data. This encouraged participation and assured employees that the data would contribute positively to inclusion goals. By adopting this approach, we ensured our data collection is respectful and impactful across diverse regions.

Through this initiative, the company encouraged employees to self-identify across multiple demographic categories that were localized by country to ensure relevance, which helped us gather accurate, inclusive data. This baseline information provided insights into the diversity of our workforce and informed inclusion strategies, helped us address specific representation gaps and build an inclusive culture based on real metrics.

DATA TRACKING SYSTEMS

Implementing a data-tracking system is crucial for effective inclusion efforts as it allows organizations to gather, monitor and analyze key diversity metrics over time. By using systems like Human Resources Information Systems (HRIS), organizations can track data related to hiring, promotions, turnover and engagement. This ensures that inclusion initiatives are not based on assumptions but on actual, reliable data. It also helps identify trends, uncover disparities and make data-driven decisions to refine strategies. Additionally, tracking systems support transparency, accountability and reporting, which are vital for maintaining organizational commitment to inclusion goals.

In addition to HRIS, organizations can use a variety of other systems to track inclusion progress. For instance, Applicant Tracking Systems (ATS) help monitor inclusion in recruitment and hiring processes. Employee Engagement Platforms, like Officevibe or Glint, collect feedback on inclusivity and team dynamics. Learning Management Systems (LMS) can track participation in inclusion training, while Performance Management Systems integrate inclusion goals into evaluations and leadership development. Workforce Analytics Tools, such as Visier or Tableau, provide deeper insights into diversity trends and help inform strategic inclusion planning.

QUALITATIVE DATA

Quantitative data provide valuable insights, but qualitative feedback brings a deeper understanding of employee experiences. Gathering qualitative feedback from employees is a critical aspect of understanding their experiences and identifying areas for improvement in inclusion efforts. This can be done through various methods such as surveys, focus groups and anonymous feedback tools. Surveys allow for a broader range of responses, while focus groups provide in-depth discussions, giving employees a platform to share personal insights and suggestions. Anonymous feedback encourages openness, ensuring employees feel comfortable sharing honest opinions about workplace culture, inclusivity and any barriers they face.

DATA REPORTING

Diversity metrics should be reviewed and reported regularly, such as quarterly or annually, to gauge progress. Reports can be shared with employees, leadership and other stakeholders to maintain transparency. This reporting process also allows organizations to celebrate successes and identify areas that need additional attention. As discussed before, inclusion is a continuous journey, and organizations should use insights from their data to refine strategies. For instance, if data reveals that certain groups are underrepresented in specific roles, organizations might strengthen recruiting or development programmes targeting these areas.

Accountability is crucial for driving meaningful progress in inclusion efforts. When inclusion goals are integrated into performance evaluations for leadership, it reinforces the message that inclusion is not just a priority, but a measurable aspect of success. Tying inclusion outcomes to compensation or bonuses where legally applicable further incentivizes leaders to actively engage in these initiatives, creating a sense of personal investment. This approach holds leaders accountable, ensuring that inclusion strategies are not only adopted but also maintained and enhanced, aligning organizational priorities with business success. Such accountability also encourages transparency, allowing employees to see the commitment from the top.

THINKING OUTSIDE THE BOX

When measuring and tracking inclusion progress, it's essential to look beyond traditional metrics such as headcount and representation. To truly understand the effectiveness of initiatives, organizations should explore new ways of capturing data on employee experiences, such as feelings of inclusion, belonging and access to growth opportunities. Looking at diversity data beyond traditional representation metrics involves examining deeper, nuanced data points that reveal insights about the experiences of different groups within the organization.

Going beyond traditional inclusion metrics involves asking questions in employee surveys that reveal underlying sentiments about inclusion and belonging. For example, if an employee answers 'yes' to the question, 'Would you leave the organization if offered a comparable job with similar pay?' this may suggest a lack of inclusion or engagement, as employees are less likely to leave a role where they feel valued and included. Other insightful questions could include:

> 'Do you feel your ideas and contributions are valued here?'
> 'Do you have equal opportunities for career advancement?'
> 'Do you feel supported by leadership in your professional growth?'
> 'Have you witnessed or experienced discrimination or bias in the workplace?'

Expanding on secondary indicators of inclusion in employee surveys is crucial for gaining a more nuanced understanding of inclusion within an organization. These questions can also further pinpoint areas where inclusion may be lacking. Feedback on how employees perceive fairness in resource allocation or leadership access also helps identify specific areas requiring attention for fostering a more inclusive environment.

Survey questions focused on recognition, fairness and belonging give organizations insights that go beyond turnover rates, helping them address deeper issues within workplace culture. By identifying patterns in responses to these types of questions, companies can make targeted adjustments to their inclusion strategies, leading to more effective and meaningful change. This approach helps to ensure that inclusion efforts are not only seen as compliance-driven but embedded in the organization's day-to-day practices and long-term goals.

Traditional surveys have been a long-standing method of capturing employee sentiment, but newer techniques, such as AI-driven sentiment analysis and real-time pulse surveys, can provide insights into how employees feel about inclusion initiatives. Machine learning models can analyze diversity trends over time, make predictions and identify patterns that might otherwise go unnoticed. This includes predicting areas at high risk for turnover among employees or identifying job roles where inclusive hiring practices could make the most impact. By adopting machine learning algorithms, organizations can set goals based on predictive insights and improve retention and satisfaction among diverse teams.

Inclusion scorecards is another way of aggregating a variety of metrics into a single, accessible report that shows how different business areas are progressing on inclusion goals. These scorecards can track metrics such as recruitment, retention and advancement by demographic groups, but they can also incorporate inclusion metrics like mentorship participation, ERG membership and responses from inclusion sentiment surveys.

Behavioural analysis can also measure how inclusive practices are in daily workflows. For example, tools like meeting analytics software can track speaking time during meetings to ensure diverse voices are heard or monitor patterns in who gets invited to key projects. Inclusion nudges are small prompts or reminders that encourage inclusive behaviours, such as rotating roles in team meetings or highlighting achievements from underrepresented team members. This creates tangible data on inclusivity in real time and can lead to adjustments in behaviour that improve equity and representation. Similar to airport 'how satisfied were you' buttons that you press after passing immigration, that capture your authentic response in real time.

Pay equity audits are also a powerful way to ensure fair compensation across demographics. These audits can reveal if employees from all genders, racial, or ethnic backgrounds are paid equitably for similar roles and experience levels. Additionally, tracking promotions, performance ratings and career progression by demographics enables organizations to see if there are disparities in advancement opportunities. By analyzing this data, companies can address barriers in promotion or compensation that may inadvertently affect underrepresented employees.

Organizations are increasingly linking inclusion metrics with business performance indicators, such as employee retention, productivity and customer satisfaction. By examining whether diverse teams lead to better innovation or whether inclusive culture correlates with lower turnover, companies can connect inclusion progress with business outcomes.

Collecting feedback through employee resource groups (ERGs) and anonymous suggestion channels helps capture insights from all diverse perspectives, particularly on how inclusion initiatives are perceived and where gaps may exist. Additionally, analyzing exit interviews can offer valuable information on why employees from certain demographics may leave the organization, highlighting potential systemic issues that need addressing in retention efforts.

Analyzing how employees collaborate across demographics can reveal whether certain groups may be isolated or excluded in workplace networks. This is valuable in large organizations where cross-functional collaboration drives innovation. Tools like organizational network analysis (ONA) can show if specific demographics or departments are more likely to work in silos and whether diverse employees have equal access to mentors or leadership networks.

REIMAGINE EMPLOYEE LIFECYCLE DATA TRACKING

Instead of only tracking the diversity of hires, analyze the inclusion of applicants at every stage of recruitment (e.g. applicants, interviews, offers). This helps identify stages where inclusion might drop off and reveal potential bias and areas to focus key interventions. Use post-interview surveys to gauge the inclusiveness of the recruitment experience, asking candidates about how they perceived fairness and respect during the process. These data provide insights into whether diverse candidates feel valued during recruitment, a critical factor in employer branding.

Measure the effectiveness of recruitment channels for all candidates to be able to access roles. For instance, if certain job boards, networks, or partnerships (e.g. HBCUs, LGBTQ+ organizations) attract more diverse candidates, these data can help optimize sourcing strategies to make sure everyone is included. Beyond tracking who stays and who leaves, frequent surveys can gauge employees' sense of belonging, psychological safety and satisfaction. These insights can reveal early warning signs of disengagement in specific demographic groups, allowing for pre-emptive actions to improve retention.

Conduct 'stay interviews' with employees to understand why they continue with the company and what aspects of the culture help them feel included is another way of tracking how included staff feel. This information can highlight practices that reinforce retention and may reveal areas to strengthen. Use predictive analytics to identify groups at higher risk of leaving based on factors like workload, engagement scores and tenure. This helps proactively address potential inclusion challenges in specific demographics before they result in turnover.

Analyze how long different demographic groups stay within specific roles or departments. Shorter tenures in particular roles might signal barriers to growth or lack of role fit, indicating areas where policies and practices need improvement. Conduct in-depth exit interviews and analyze feedback to understand systemic issues. Identify trends in why certain groups may leave sooner or more frequently than others.

Track tenure along with lateral moves within the organization. If certain demographics make fewer lateral or cross-departmental moves, it may indicate informal barriers to growth that impact tenure. Go beyond tracking attendance; assess if development opportunities are equitably accessed across demographic groups. This includes measuring participation in stretch assignments, mentoring programmes and leadership training to see if all groups have equal opportunities.

Use skills assessments or post-training evaluations to measure how effective development programmes are across different groups. If certain groups report a lower perceived benefit, this feedback can guide adjustments in content or delivery. Track whether diverse employees receive opportunities for skill-building projects, exposure and mentoring that make them 'promotion-ready' over time. Tracking these indicators helps highlight disparities in development that may impact advancement.

Measure how long it takes employees from different backgrounds to be promoted compared to other groups. If certain employees progress at slower rates, this can signal biases in promotion criteria, informal barriers, or lack of sponsorship. Examine performance ratings across demographics to ensure consistency. This involves reviewing rating trends, comments and any discrepancies that suggest biased performance assessments.

Measure inclusion outcomes under individual managers by analyzing the diversity of teams, turnover rates and promotion rates for direct reports. Managers with strong inclusion outcomes can be studied as role models, while others may benefit from inclusion-based training.

Tracking inclusion metrics in these areas offers a holistic view of the employee experience, capturing insights that go beyond demographic representation. By integrating qualitative data from surveys and interviews, real-time feedback and performance analytics, organizations can better understand the systemic factors that impact inclusion outcomes and continuously improve inclusivity across the employee lifecycle. This approach ensures that inclusion efforts create meaningful, sustained impact on culture and business success.

By adopting some of these more advanced methods, organizations can track inclusion in a comprehensive, innovative and actionable way. This approach ensures that inclusion goals are measurable, relevant and aligned with both employee well-being and business success, supporting a more inclusive workplace culture.

INTEGRATING INCLUSION MEASUREMENT INTO ORGANIZATIONAL CULTURE

To embed inclusion measurement into the organizational culture, leaders must foster an environment where accountability is valued, transparency is prioritized, and inclusion is a shared responsibility. Organizations can achieve this by openly discussing inclusion goals and progress in company meetings, setting inclusion milestones as part of strategic planning, and celebrating inclusion achievements with the same enthusiasm as business successes.

By weaving inclusion measurement into the fabric of an organization's operations, companies can create a workplace where every individual feels valued, supported and empowered. This level of integration not only drives equitable outcomes but also strengthens the organization's reputation as an employer of choice.

In sum, measuring inclusion progress is not a one-time task; it's an ongoing commitment. Organizations that invest in robust inclusion tracking systems, share data transparently and remain flexible to iterate on strategies are better positioned to create meaningful and sustainable changes. These actions serve as the foundation for a diverse, equitable and inclusive workplace where everyone can thrive.

8

EMBEDDING INCLUSION INTO EVERY STAGE OF THE EMPLOYEE LIFECYCLE

Embedding inclusion at each stage of the employee lifecycle, is fundamental to creating a truly inclusive workplace where all employees can thrive. Each phase – attraction, recruitment, onboarding, development, retention and offboarding – provides an opportunity to integrate practices that foster inclusivity. When inclusion principles are consistently applied across the entire employee lifecycle, organizations are more likely to experience enhanced employee engagement, improved innovation and better business outcomes.

The attraction phase is the starting point where an organization makes its first impression on potential candidates. It's essential to ensure that recruitment messaging and employer branding reflect a commitment to inclusion for all groups. Job descriptions should be written in inclusive language, ensuring they don't unintentionally exclude certain groups. This might include eliminating gendered language or focusing on required skills instead of qualifications that may disproportionately disadvantage certain demographics. Additionally, broadening the recruitment outreach to non-traditional sources – such as diverse professional networks, universities and community organizations – helps attract candidates from a variety of backgrounds. By making inclusion a visible part of the employer brand, organizations signal to prospective employees that they value diversity, making it more likely that all individuals will apply.

Once candidates are attracted to the organization, the recruitment process must be designed to reduce bias and increase fairness. Blind recruitment, where identifying information such as names and genders are removed, is one way to mitigate unconscious bias in hiring. Using structured interviews, where each candidate is asked the same set of questions, ensures a more equitable process. Additionally, recruiting from a diverse range of sources ensures that the candidate pool itself reflects the diversity the organization seeks. Having a diverse hiring panel can also help ensure that multiple perspectives are considered, reducing the likelihood of bias influencing hiring decisions.

The onboarding stage is another critical touchpoint for embedding inclusion within the organization. New hires should feel welcomed, valued and integrated into a culture that celebrates inclusion. During onboarding, it's important to provide inclusion training that covers topics such as unconscious bias, cultural competency and the organization's commitment to inclusion. Employee resource groups (ERGs) can also be introduced at this stage to help new hires connect with communities within the company that share similar backgrounds or experiences. A well-structured, inclusive onboarding experience sets the tone for how new employees will experience their time at the organization.

As employees settle into their roles, the development phase plays a key role in reinforcing inclusion. It's important to provide equitable access to career development opportunities for all employees, regardless of their background. This includes providing mentorship and sponsorship opportunities, ensuring that performance evaluations are free from bias and offering leadership training that prepares employees for senior roles. By creating an environment where all employees have the resources and support they need to grow, organizations demonstrate their commitment to ensuring that everyone has a fair chance to succeed.

Equally important is the retention phase, where inclusion initiatives must focus on creating a workplace culture that makes all employees feel supported and included. This means creating policies that promote work-life balance, offering benefits that meet the needs of all employees (e.g. flexible work arrangements, mental health support), and ensuring that underrepresented groups are not only welcomed but also have a voice in decision-making processes. Regular surveys and feedback mechanisms should be implemented to assess employee satisfaction and organizations should act on the data gathered to address areas of concern. This continuous feedback loop helps identify any systemic issues within the organization and allows for swift action to be taken to address them.

Finally, the offboarding process offers an opportunity to gather valuable insights. When employees leave, exit interviews should focus on understanding their experiences with inclusion within the organization. Feedback about the company's culture, opportunities for growth and challenges faced can provide important data that helps inform future inclusion efforts. Departing employees may be more open in sharing their experiences, providing organizations with honest insights into areas that need improvement. This reflection ensures that inclusion initiatives are constantly evolving and adapting to meet the needs of all employees.

When inclusion is embedded at every stage of the employee lifecycle, organizations ensure that all employees, regardless of their background, feel empowered to contribute, develop and succeed. By integrating inclusion principles into attraction, recruitment, onboarding, development, retention and offboarding, organizations foster a culture where inclusion is not only valued but actively promoted. This not only helps attract top talent from diverse backgrounds but also ensures that employees remain engaged, feel a sense of belonging and have equal opportunities for advancement. Research shows that inclusive organizations are more innovative, make better decisions and achieve better financial results. Therefore, by embedding inclusion throughout the employee lifecycle, organizations not only support their employees but also position themselves for long-term success.

ATTRACTION

To embed inclusion in the attraction process of a company, it's essential to prioritize inclusivity from the first interaction a candidate has with the brand. This can be achieved by creating diverse and welcoming job advertisements, establishing fair hiring practices and leveraging inclusive language and imagery in recruitment materials. Using inclusive language ensures that job descriptions appeal to a wide array of potential applicants, avoiding gendered language, jargon or phrases that may deter qualified candidates from certain backgrounds. Job descriptions should also emphasize the organization's commitment to inclusion, which can signal to candidates that they would be entering an inclusive environment.

Broadening recruitment channels is another important aspect of the attraction process. Expanding beyond traditional networks to include job boards, career fairs and professional associations that cater to diverse populations helps to reach a wider range of potential candidates. Partnering with organizations that focus on the career development of specific groups, such as women in STEM, veterans, or individuals with disabilities, is an effective way to diversify the candidate pool. Additionally, offering internship or apprenticeship programmes for underrepresented groups can help attract talent early and build a pipeline for future recruitment.

Ensuring that all recruiting materials visually reflect the diversity of the company is also crucial. When candidates see themselves represented in promotional materials, social media content, or company websites, it can foster a sense of belonging and make them more likely to engage with the organization. Current employees' stories, testimonials and profiles can showcase the company's inclusive culture, highlighting support systems like ERGs and mentorship programmes. Emphasizing the ways in which inclusion is woven into the fabric of the organization, such as through mentorship opportunities and professional development for all backgrounds, can enhance the appeal of the company as a place where diverse talent is valued and supported.

RECRUITMENT AND HIRING

The recruitment process plays a pivotal role in shaping an organization's commitment to inclusion. Establishing equitable hiring practices ensures that opportunities are accessible to individuals from diverse backgrounds, fostering a workforce that embodies a range of experiences and perspectives. Each stage of the recruitment process, from crafting job descriptions to interviews, offers an opportunity to embed inclusion principles thoughtfully.

Creating inclusive job descriptions is the first step in attracting a diverse pool of candidates. It's essential to use language that avoids bias, such as overly masculine-coded terms or unnecessarily rigid requirements that might deter qualified individuals. For example, instead of listing exhaustive 'ideal' qualifications, focus on the essential skills and competencies needed for the role. Tools like Textio can help organizations identify and remove biased language in job postings, ensuring the descriptions resonate with a broader audience.

Implement blind recruitment practices designed to minimize unconscious bias in hiring by anonymizing certain details in a candidate's application, such as their name, gender, age, ethnicity and even education or address, depending on the level of detail being removed. By withholding this information, hiring managers and recruiters are encouraged to focus solely on a candidate's qualifications, skills and relevant experience, rather than being influenced – intentionally or unintentionally – by factors unrelated to job performance.

The interview process is a key moment to ensure objectivity and fairness. Structured interviews, where all candidates are asked the same set of questions, help reduce opportunities for bias to influence decisions. Training interviewers to recognize and mitigate unconscious biases is equally essential, ensuring evaluations are based on skills and potential rather than personal assumptions. Using diverse hiring panels further enhances fairness by incorporating varied perspectives into candidate evaluations, reducing the likelihood of individual biases affecting decisions.

Organizations can make their hiring decisions more equitable by prioritizing transparency and using standardized, skills-based assessments. By focusing on 'cultural add' rather than 'cultural fit,' organizations can shift the emphasis from selecting candidates who feel familiar to those who bring a different perspective.

ONBOARDING

The onboarding process is a pivotal stage where new hires gain their initial understanding of an organization's culture and values. By embedding inclusion principles at this stage, organizations not only reinforce their commitment to these ideals but also create an environment where new employees feel welcomed, valued and equipped to thrive. A thoughtful approach to inclusion during onboarding ensures that employees start their journey with a clear understanding of the company's dedication to inclusivity and respect.

One essential component of inclusive onboarding is providing inclusion-focused training. This training should cover topics like unconscious bias, inclusive communication and the organization's specific inclusion policies and goals. By addressing unconscious biases, employees can become more aware of how biases may influence their perceptions and interactions, fostering a culture of self-reflection and growth. Inclusive communication training, on the other hand, equips employees to work effectively in diverse teams by emphasizing respect and understanding of cultural differences. Sharing the company's inclusion commitments during onboarding ensures that new hires understand the organization's vision and their role in achieving it.

ERGs also play a critical role in the onboarding process. Introducing new hires to ERGs creates a sense of immediate belonging by connecting them to networks of peers with shared experiences or identities. These groups offer professional development opportunities, support networks and a platform for underrepresented employees to have their voices heard, as well as a safe space for those who want to be allies to learn and grow.

Beyond training and ERGs, organizations can enhance inclusion in onboarding through mentorship and buddy programmes. Pairing new hires with mentors who can provide guidance and insight into organizational culture can be especially valuable for employees from underrepresented backgrounds. Additionally, making onboarding materials and processes accessible to individuals with disabilities demonstrates a commitment to equity. Customizing onboarding experiences to meet the diverse needs of new hires further reinforces this commitment, signalling that the organization values individual differences.

Embedding inclusion in onboarding not only helps to create an inclusive environment but also contributes to long-term success by boosting employee retention and satisfaction. New employees who feel valued and supported are more likely to contribute their unique perspectives and thrive within the organization. By prioritizing inclusion at the outset, companies position themselves as inclusive and forward-thinking employers, enhancing their reputation and ability to attract top talent across all demographics.

DEVELOPMENT AND RETENTION

As employees settle into their roles, organizations must implement strategies that prioritize retention and career development through the lens of equity. This ensures that all employees, regardless of their background, feel valued, supported and empowered to grow within the company. Organizations that focus on equity in retention and development not only improve employee satisfaction and loyalty but also enhance overall performance by leveraging the diverse potential of their workforce.

Equity in career development involves identifying and addressing systemic barriers that may prevent employees from underrepresented groups from advancing. Organizations should provide clear and accessible career pathways, ensuring that opportunities for promotions, training and leadership roles are distributed fairly. For example, companies can implement mentorship or sponsorship programmes that pair employees with senior leaders to provide guidance, visibility and advocacy.

Offering tailored training and development programmes is another key element. Organizations should assess the specific needs of their workforce and develop programmes that address gaps in skills or experiences that may exist due to inequities in access to resources. For instance, providing leadership development programmes for women or creating technical training initiatives for underrepresented groups in tech roles can help level the playing field in countries where it is legal to do so. These initiatives not only prepare employees for future roles but also demonstrate the organization's commitment to their growth.

One key area is mentorship and sponsorship programmes targeted towards underrepresented groups in countries where it is legal to do so. By pairing employees with mentors who understand their unique challenges, organizations create a supportive structure that allows diverse talent to navigate career paths more effectively. Additionally, sponsors – often leaders or managers who can advocate for their mentees' advancement – play a critical role in opening up opportunities for growth and leadership that may otherwise be inaccessible.

Equitable access to development resources is also crucial. Companies should ensure that all employees have equal access to professional development opportunities, such as skills training, leadership development workshops and continuing education. This can help bridge gaps in knowledge and skill levels, enabling a more level playing field where diverse employees can advance at similar rates.

To ensure equity, organizations must also reassess their feedback and performance evaluation systems. Bias in these systems can hinder the advancement of certain groups. Using standardized, transparent criteria for evaluations and offering training for managers on conscious inclusion can promote fairness. Regular 360-degree feedback mechanisms, where peers, subordinates and supervisors provide input, can also provide a holistic and unbiased view of an employee's performance.

Recognizing and celebrating the contributions of employees from all backgrounds is essential for fostering equity. Organizations can create equitable reward systems that ensure all employees have equal access to recognition, from awards programmes to salary increases. Transparency in pay practices, through pay equity audits, ensures that all employees feel valued for their work.

Regularly conduct pay equity audits to ensure that there are no pay disparities across gender, race and other demographic categories. Addressing any gaps found through audits is essential to ensure equity within the organization and demonstrate a commitment to fair compensation practices.

Moreover, embedding inclusion in succession planning and performance evaluations allows companies to actively support diverse leadership pipelines. Organizations should make a conscious effort to assess and remove biases in performance reviews, ensuring evaluations are consistent and focused on objective performance indicators. By doing so, companies enable equitable promotion practices that are based on merit and potential rather than background or existing networks. Initiatives such as standardized performance rubrics and inclusion review committees can help to identify and address potential biases in the advancement process.

Lastly, building a culture of recognition and retention for all talent means creating a work environment that celebrates differences and provides continuous support. Recognition programmes that celebrate cultural diversity, achievements and contributions from all backgrounds help employees feel valued. Regular feedback and retention interviews can identify areas where employees may feel unsupported, and proactive engagement with their concerns allows organizations to refine their inclusion efforts and create a genuinely inclusive culture.

By embedding these inclusion principles in development and retention strategies, companies can create a more inclusive environment that attracts, supports and retains all talent. This commitment not only fosters employee satisfaction and productivity but also positions the company as a leader in inclusivity, benefiting long-term performance and innovation.

PERFORMANCE MANAGEMENT

Performance management processes are critical for fostering inclusion within an organization. These systems, when designed thoughtfully, ensure that all employees are evaluated and rewarded fairly, and they contribute to a workplace culture where everyone feels valued and empowered to succeed.

Performance management systems must employ consistent, objective criteria to evaluate employees. Subjective or vague standards can introduce unconscious bias, disproportionately affecting employees from certain groups. Organizations should develop clear, role-specific benchmarks tied to measurable outcomes. For example, instead of rating an employee on 'leadership potential' without context, a criterion might assess their ability to lead successful cross-functional projects within a given timeframe.

To promote equity, performance goals should be clear, measurable and collaboratively developed between managers and employees. When designing these goals, consider each employee's role and unique contributions, allowing flexibility in how they achieve their objectives. For example, rather than only rewarding traditional forms of leadership (such as public speaking or visibility in meetings), value other forms of contribution like collaboration, mentorship and innovation that might otherwise go unnoticed. Including inclusion-related competencies, like cross-cultural communication and collaboration, as part of the performance expectations can further emphasize the value of inclusive behaviours and encourage employees to develop these skills actively.

Managers play a central role in performance evaluations and must be equipped to recognize and mitigate bias. Unconscious biases – such as affinity bias or stereotypes – can inadvertently influence assessments, leading to inequitable outcomes. Training managers to identify and address these biases ensures that all employees are judged fairly.

Using 360-degree feedback processes can help mitigate individual biases by gathering input from multiple sources, such as peers, subordinates and supervisors. This method ensures a more holistic and equitable evaluation of an employee's contributions. Diverse feedback channels capture a fuller picture of an employee's impact, reducing the potential for any single individual's biases to dominate.

Performance management should include equitable goal-setting practices. Employees should have access to the same opportunities for professional growth, and goals should be tailored to their roles and career aspirations. For example, employees from underrepresented groups should not be disproportionately tasked with 'invisible work' like cultural initiatives or diversity efforts unless these contributions are explicitly valued and rewarded within the performance system.

To promote equity, rewards and promotions must be based on transparent criteria. Pay equity audits, help identify disparities in compensation linked to race, gender, or other factors. Similarly, ensuring that promotions are not influenced by favouritism or bias requires consistent processes that prioritize merit and potential over subjective impressions.

Holding regular calibration sessions, where managers discuss and align their evaluations across teams, ensures fairness. These sessions help identify and address discrepancies in how performance standards are applied, fostering a consistent approach throughout the organization. Engaging employees in the design and refinement of performance management processes helps build trust and inclusion. Employees should have the opportunity to provide feedback on how they are evaluated and the perceived fairness of the system. Open dialogue promotes transparency and demonstrates a commitment to continuous improvement.

Organizations must track key metrics to measure the equity of their performance management processes. Metrics might include promotion rates, performance scores and pay adjustments across different demographic groups. By analyzing this data, companies can identify trends or inequities and take proactive steps to address them.

When performance management systems are designed with equity and inclusion in mind, they not only create a more fair and supportive environment but also drive organizational success. Equitable systems motivate employees, reduce turnover and foster a culture where everyone can contribute their best work, ultimately benefiting both individuals and the organization as a whole.

EMPLOYEE ENGAGEMENT AND WELL-BEING

Employee well-being is a cornerstone of successful inclusion programmes. When employees feel included, respected and valued, their sense of well-being improves, which directly impacts their engagement, productivity and overall satisfaction within the workplace. Embedding inclusion in a company's approach to wellbeing is essential for fostering a truly inclusive environment where all employees feel supported, valued and able to thrive. This begins with designing wellness programmes that are sensitive to diverse needs across backgrounds, lifestyles and personal challenges.

Access to equitable resources, such as mental health services, professional development opportunities and ergonomic tools, is vital for employee well-being. Inclusion programmes that identify and address gaps in access, such as providing culturally sensitive mental health counselling, healthcare benefits that cover mental health or services specific to LGBTQ+ employees or accommodating employees with disabilities, demonstrate an organization's commitment to equity.

Inclusion initiatives often focus on policies that respect diverse life circumstances, which is directly linked to employee well-being. Flexible work arrangements, parental leave and caregiver support policies are examples of inclusion driven strategies that enable employees to balance professional and personal responsibilities. Organizations that implement these policies show respect for their employees' diverse needs, reducing burnout and improving mental and physical health.

Inclusion programmes that foster community building contribute to emotional well-being by reducing feelings of isolation. Initiatives like ERGs, company-sponsored social events, or mentoring relationships can create spaces where employees form meaningful connections. These efforts are particularly impactful for employees from underrepresented groups, who may otherwise feel excluded in less diverse environments.

Create a safe and supportive environment for employees to speak about mental health issues. Promote an organizational culture that destigmatizes seeking help and provides access to mental health resources, especially for employees from historically marginalized groups who may face additional stressors.

Finally, embedding inclusion into wellbeing means fostering a culture of psychological safety where all employees feel comfortable discussing their health and wellbeing needs without fear of stigma or reprisal. Managers should be trained in empathy, cultural competence and bias awareness to support diverse wellbeing needs effectively. Regular assessments of wellness programmes through employee feedback and data analysis ensure that these initiatives remain relevant, responsive and inclusive as the workforce evolves. A strong, inclusion driven approach to wellbeing not only promotes individual employee satisfaction but also strengthens organizational resilience and engagement, creating a workplace where all can contribute fully.

EXIT AND OFFBOARDING

The final stage of the employee lifecycle, offboarding, presents a unique opportunity for organizations to gather valuable insights that can improve inclusion efforts. Departing employees, particularly those from underrepresented groups, can offer critical feedback on the organization's culture, practices and policies. Leveraging this feedback can help identify systemic issues and opportunities for growth that may not be visible during an employee's tenure.

Exit interviews are a vital tool for understanding the experiences of departing employees. Organizations should design these interviews to include open-ended questions focused on inclusion-related topics, such as inclusivity in team dynamics, fairness in performance evaluations and the accessibility of growth opportunities. For example, questions like 'Did you feel supported in your career development?' or 'Were there any barriers to your success?' can uncover patterns that point to inequities in the workplace.

To ensure candid responses, it is essential to establish a safe and confidential environment for exit interviews. Employees are more likely to share honest feedback if they feel that their input will not lead to retaliation or negative consequences. Using third-party services to conduct exit interviews or providing anonymous survey options can encourage more transparency. It is also important to communicate how the organization plans to use this feedback to drive change, signalling a genuine commitment to improvement.

Collecting data from exit interviews over time allows organizations to identify trends and patterns that might indicate larger systemic issues. For instance, if multiple employees from a specific demographic cite a lack of career advancement opportunities or feelings of exclusion, this could point to biases within leadership or structural inequities that need addressing. By analyzing this data, companies can refine inclusion initiatives to target these specific areas.

Offboarding is not just about learning from what went wrong; it is also an opportunity to celebrate what worked well. Positive feedback from departing employees can highlight strengths in the organization's inclusion practices, providing a roadmap for areas to amplify and replicate. This dual approach ensures that offboarding contributes to continuous improvement across the employee lifecycle.

Developing alumni networks for employees who have left the organization is a great way to provide ex-employees with an opportunity to maintain relationships with former employees, receive ongoing feedback about the company's culture, and potentially bring back talent from diverse backgrounds in the future.

How an organization handles offboarding can significantly impact its reputation. A transparent and respectful offboarding process demonstrates a commitment to treating employees equitably, even as they exit. This can lead to positive word-of-mouth referrals, a stronger employer brand and a more inclusive image that attracts talent in the future or help employees 'boomeranging back'.

By viewing offboarding as a critical phase of the employee lifecycle, organizations can transform what is often seen as the end of the employee relationship into a springboard for meaningful inclusion advancements. The insights gained from departing employees, when coupled with a commitment to action, can drive systemic improvements that benefit the entire organization.

Embedding inclusion at each stage of the employee lifecycle not only helps create a more inclusive and equitable work environment but also contributes to the broader business goals of talent attraction, employee retention and performance. By integrating inclusion principles into recruitment, onboarding, development, performance management, engagement and offboarding, organizations can ensure that inclusion is woven into the fabric of every employee's experience. This systemic approach helps build an environment where every employee feels valued, respected and empowered to contribute, ultimately driving better business outcomes.

9

NAVIGATING CHALLENGES: ADDRESSING RESISTANCE AND BARRIERS

Navigating challenges related to inclusion is essential for organizations seeking to implement meaningful change. Addressing resistance and barriers is crucial because these challenges can impede progress and undermine efforts to create an inclusive environment. Organizations must recognize that resistance often stems from fear of change, a lack of understanding, or ingrained biases. By proactively addressing these challenges, leaders can foster a culture of openness and acceptance, which is vital for inclusion initiatives to thrive.

Resistance to inclusion initiatives may manifest in various forms, such as skepticism, indifference, or outright opposition. Understanding the underlying reasons for this resistance is critical. For example, research shows that individuals may feel threatened by changes that challenge their beliefs or privilege. By engaging in open dialogues that explore these concerns, organizations can demystify inclusion efforts and create a safe space for employees to express their thoughts. This approach not only encourages buy-in but also helps dispel myths surrounding diversity initiatives.

When organizations adopt inclusion initiatives, some individuals may feel that these changes threaten their power or position within the workplace. This can lead to a sense of entitlement being challenged, prompting defensive reactions and understanding of inclusion Objectives. In some cases, backlash can stem from a lack of understanding regarding the goals of inclusion programmes. Employees or stakeholders may view these initiatives as merely performative or tokenistic, leading to doubt and resistance.

In today's politically charged environment, discussions around diversity and inclusion can become highly contentious. Individuals may align their views with broader political ideologies, leading to backlash against perceived 'woke' agendas or policies. Some companies that have made public commitments to inclusion have faced backlash from segments of their customer base. For example, brands have encountered significant criticism for their advertising campaigns focused on social issues, which some consumers perceived as overly political.

One of the primary sources of external resistance is societal attitudes towards diversity and inclusion. For instance, groups that feel threatened by changing demographics or shifting power dynamics may actively oppose initiatives perceived as favouring minority groups. This phenomenon is often exacerbated by political discourse and media representation, which can influence public perceptions of inclusion. Organizations may face backlash from communities or customers who view inclusion initiatives as unnecessary or as an infringement on traditional values.

Another significant external barrier comes from regulatory and policy frameworks. In some cases, organizations may encounter legal challenges or inconsistencies in compliance related to inclusion efforts. For example, laws governing affirmative action or equal opportunity may vary widely across jurisdictions, creating uncertainty about how to implement inclusive practices. Furthermore, businesses operating globally must navigate diverse regulatory environments, which can complicate efforts to standardize inclusion initiatives across different markets.

Stakeholder expectations also play a crucial role in shaping external resistance. Investors, customers and community groups increasingly expect companies to demonstrate a commitment to inclusion. However, if organizations are perceived as merely performing diversity without genuine investment, they risk alienating these stakeholders. Studies have shown that customers are more likely to support brands that align with their values, including those related to social justice and equity. Thus, if a company's inclusion efforts are seen as superficial or insincere, it may face backlash from consumers who prioritize authenticity in brand messaging.

ADDRESSING INCLUSION RESISTANCE INTERNALLY

Organizations should strive to communicate the purpose and benefits of inclusion initiatives clearly. Engaging stakeholders in open dialogues can foster understanding and reduce resistance. Actively involving employees from all backgrounds in the planning and implementation of inclusion initiatives can help mitigate backlash. This participation ensures that programmes are relevant and considerate of various perspectives. Regularly assessing and sharing the outcome of initiatives can help demonstrate their effectiveness and address concerns about tokenism or ineffectiveness. This transparency can build trust and support for ongoing efforts.

While DEI backlash is a significant challenge, understanding implications can help organizations navigate these complexities effectively. By promoting clear communication, inclusive practices and measurable outcomes, organizations can not only mitigate backlash but also create a more engaged and supportive environment for diversity, and inclusion.

Organizations can implement strategies to navigate these challenges effectively. First, providing comprehensive education and training on inclusion can equip employees with the knowledge necessary to understand its importance and benefits. Training should address implicit biases, cultural competencies and the business case for diversity. Additionally, leveraging data to highlight the positive impact of inclusion on performance and innovation can help counter resistance by demonstrating tangible benefits.

Building a coalition of allies within the organization can also mitigate resistance. Leaders should identify and empower individuals who are passionate about inclusion to champion these efforts. When employees see their peers actively supporting inclusion initiatives, it can shift the organizational culture and reduce barriers. Engaging in collaborative efforts with employee resource groups (ERGs) allows organizations to gather diverse perspectives, further enriching the inclusion conversation and fostering a sense of belonging.

Understanding the organizational culture is vital to identify areas resistant to inclusion efforts. Surveys, focus groups and tools like the *Organizational Culture Inventory* can uncover employee attitudes, pinpointing issues like unconscious biases or a lack of understanding about the importance of inclusion. For example, a survey might reveal that employees feel excluded in decision-making, which informs targeted initiatives.

Communicating inclusively within an organization is crucial for fostering a welcoming, diverse and supportive environment. When employees feel respected and valued in their interactions, it enhances engagement, improves morale and leads to better organizational outcomes. Below are several key strategies for communicating inclusively internally:

Inclusive language avoids terms that may unintentionally exclude, offend, or stereotype individuals based on their gender, race, disability, or other identities. Inclusive communication also involves genuinely listening to employees' concerns, perspectives and ideas. Active listening requires leaders and teams to focus not just on hearing words but on understanding the context and emotions behind them. This means asking open-ended questions, reflecting on what is said, and making sure every voice is heard.

Empathy in communication means understanding and validating others' emotions and experiences. Leaders and team members should model empathetic behaviour by acknowledging the diverse backgrounds and experiences of their colleagues. This could mean acknowledging the unique challenges faced by different groups and offering support accordingly. Encouraging open dialogue about inclusion helps employees feel comfortable discussing sensitive topics. This can be achieved through regular inclusion-focused town halls, employee forums, or anonymous surveys where employees can share their thoughts without fear of retaliation.

Transparency builds trust and ensures that everyone is on the same page regarding inclusion initiatives. Share the reasoning behind the company's commitment to inclusion, progress towards goals and the impact of those efforts. Utilising active leadership involvement that can help set the tone around inclusion for the organization.

Finally, it is essential to recognize that overcoming resistance and barriers is an ongoing process. Regularly assessing the impact of inclusion initiatives through feedback loops, surveys and performance metrics ensures that organizations remain responsive to employees' concerns and needs. By committing to continuous improvement and demonstrating a genuine investment in inclusion, organizations can create a culture that not only tolerates diversity but embraces it as a strength.

STRATEGIES TO OVERCOME EXTERNAL RESISTANCE

Proactively initiating open conversations with stakeholders such as community leaders, customers and investors can help address concerns and align expectations. For example, an organization expanding into a conservative community might host listening sessions with local leaders to explain how its inclusion efforts align with shared values like fairness and opportunity. These dialogues build trust and reduce apprehension about the organization's inclusion goals.

Sharing clear and honest updates about inclusion progress demonstrates an organization's commitment to meaningful change. Regular reports that outline both achievements and areas needing improvement foster credibility. For instance, an organization publishing quarterly inclusion progress reports, including workforce demographics and retention trends, can show its stakeholders its dedication to transparency and accountability.

Forming alliances with advocacy groups and other organizations strengthens inclusion initiatives and provides additional credibility. For example, an organization partnering with a nonprofit to diversify its talent pipeline can demonstrate a genuine commitment to equity and inclusion. Such partnerships can also help combat external resistance by amplifying shared goals and promoting a unified message.

Use social media platforms to highlight inclusion initiatives and success stories. Engaging content can counter negative perceptions and build a positive brand image. Keep abreast of social movements and public sentiment regarding inclusion. Organizations should be prepared to respond to emerging issues and adapt their strategies accordingly.

Providing resources that address misconceptions about inclusion helps shift public attitudes and reduce resistance. Offering community workshops or investor briefings on the economic and social benefits of inclusive practices can transform sceptics into supporters. For instance, an organization launching public webinars on the connection between diversity and innovation can help stakeholders understand the tangible benefits of inclusion.

By addressing external resistance and barriers thoughtfully, organizations can create a more conducive environment for inclusion initiatives to thrive. A proactive approach that involves stakeholder engagement, transparency and education is essential for overcoming these challenges and achieving long-lasting systemic change.

LEADERSHIP APPROACH NEEDED

Leaders must first understand the political, social and legal environments in which their organizations operate. While some regions may experience an outward push against inclusion initiatives – through legislation or social movements – others may embrace and push for more inclusive practices. Companies operating across multiple geographies must be prepared to adapt their strategies based on local dynamics, which may include navigating varying levels of governmental support for inclusion, public sentiment and even stakeholder influence.

Leaders can adopt internal-only strategies to safeguard employees from external political pressures. This could mean focusing on fostering an inclusive culture internally, providing safe spaces for underrepresented groups and ensuring that employees feel supported within the company's boundaries. While this approach can be effective in the short term, it may not lead to long-term impact or alignment with evolving societal norms.

Alternatively, leaders can take a more active stance on inclusion, advocating for systemic change beyond the workplace, even in the face of backlash. This approach has the potential to deepen employee loyalty, particularly among younger generations who are more vocal about their expectations for corporate responsibility. According to research from Cornell University's ILR School, inclusion advocacy – when strategically feasible – can demonstrate corporate leadership and align with the growing societal demand for accountability. Such actions may include participating in social justice movements, publicly supporting inclusion-related policy changes, or leading initiatives that push for legislative change.

The future of inclusion will likely require companies to navigate shifting political and social climates. As policies evolve and public sentiment fluctuates, Inclusive leaders must remain agile, reassessing their strategies and adjusting accordingly. Being flexible is crucial, organizations should be prepared to pivot between internal-only approaches and external advocacy, depending on the broader environment. However, a consistent commitment to core inclusion values must always remain at the heart of these efforts, regardless of external challenges.

To successfully navigate the changing climate, leaders must develop a robust strategic framework that allows them to pivot based on local needs and global shifts. By balancing internal initiatives with external advocacy when possible, and always remaining grounded in core values, Inclusive leaders can ensure that their organizations not only survive backlash but thrive through it. In doing so, they'll reinforce their reputation as leaders in social responsibility and organizational inclusivity, even amid turbulent political climates.

WHAT TO CALL DEI?

The debate over renaming DEI initiatives or teams within organizations has become a timely discussion as companies seek to adapt to changing, legal and social dynamics while continuing to deepen employee engagement. Changing the DEI name is a strategic decision with both pros and cons, and organizations should carefully consider these aspects before making a shift.

1. Pros of Renaming DEI

Some employees and stakeholders may view the term 'DEI' as narrow or overly focused on compliance. Renaming DEI to terms that emphasize 'Belonging', 'Accessibility' or 'Culture' could increase buy-in by creating a sense that the programme focuses on the whole workforce, not just specific groups. Many companies have recently shifted to using 'inclusion' to reflect a broader, more inclusive organizational focus, which has helped increase engagement across all groups.

Changing the name can help align the initiative more closely with the company's culture and brand values. Organizations that emphasize innovation, for example, may choose terms that convey openness and collaboration, such as 'Diversity, inclusion, and Innovation'. This alignment can help employees see DEI efforts as an intrinsic part of the company's identity rather than a standalone programme.

The term 'DEI' has, for some, taken on political connotations, leading to resistance or backlash from groups within or outside the organization. Renaming the initiative to something like 'People & Culture', 'Inclusion & Belonging' or 'Empowerment & Engagement' can mitigate some of this resistance and make it feel more approachable.

The traditional inclusion model primarily focusses on diversity of identities (e.g. race, gender), but many organizations are evolving towards an expanded view that includes diversity of thought, backgrounds, experiences and abilities. Renaming the programme to reflect these broader considerations can signal an inclusive focus that extends beyond demographic characteristics.

Renaming DEI can help shift focus from compliance-based programmes to a more universal, people-centred approach. For example, words like 'empowerment', 'growth' or 'respect' can convey a focus on benefiting all employees, reducing the perception that these initiatives serve only specific groups. This reframing makes it clear that inclusion efforts aim to improve experiences and outcomes for the entire workforce, reinforcing a sense of shared purpose and collective benefit

2. Cons of Renaming DEI

A name change can sometimes water down the focus on core DEI principles like racial, gender and economic equity. By expanding or shifting the terminology, there is a risk that specific, necessary work on systemic issues like racial justice or gender equity could lose its sense of urgency or visibility.

If DEI has been a longstanding part of an organization's identity, renaming it could create confusion and disengagement among employees, especially those already invested in DEI work. To avoid misunderstandings, organizations would need clear communication on why the change is happening and how it continues to support key goals.

DEI is a widely recognized acronym, both within organizations and across industries. By moving away from this established term, a company risks losing the external credibility and internal momentum that comes with it. For example, DEI initiatives often connect with external standards and benchmarks, and changing the term may lead to misalignment or perceived inauthenticity.

A name change would require an organization-wide campaign to explain the rationale, updated goals and focus areas. It can take significant time and resources to ensure employees understand and embrace the new terminology and vision.

3. Balancing Pros and Cons in Decision-Making

For organizations considering renaming their DEI department, it is crucial to evaluate how a new term might align with the company's goals, mission and employee engagement. Conducting surveys or focus groups to gather employee perspectives can also provide valuable insight and foster transparency. Additionally, leadership should ensure that any new terminology does not dilute the programme's commitment to meaningful equity and inclusion work, especially for groups that have historically faced barriers. Ultimately, the decision should balance clarity, inclusivity and alignment with organizational culture to ensure that inclusion work remains focused, impactful and widely embraced.

While DEI backlash presents a challenge, it also offers an opportunity for organizations to engage in open dialogue, educate their workforce and build a more inclusive culture. By fostering a mindset of learning, transparency and inclusion, companies can overcome resistance and continue to drive meaningful change. The future of inclusion lies in creating a sustainable environment where all voices are heard and valued, and where progress is measured not just in numbers but in cultural transformation.

FUTURE INCLUSION ENGAGEMENT FRAMEWORKS

As organizations look ahead to the future of inclusion in an increasingly globalized and politically polarized world, the development of adaptable and responsive frameworks is essential to ensure lasting impact. The effectiveness of inclusion strategies is no longer solely reliant on the organizational level but must also account for the rapidly changing dynamics across different regions, cultures and political climates. Therefore, inclusion frameworks of the future should focus on adaptability, cultural awareness and scalability, while still upholding universal values such as equity, fairness and respect for diversity.

One key element of future inclusion engagement frameworks is **context-awareness**. A framework that works in one region may not be suitable in another due to differences in local customs, societal norms or legal requirements. For example, certain diversity measures that are common in North America or Western Europe, such as affirmative action or gender quotas, may be viewed differently or even face legal challenges in other regions. To address this, future frameworks must be adaptable to specific local environments, taking into account cultural values, historical context and regional political dynamics. This could include modifying policies to reflect local traditions, while still promoting core inclusion objectives.

Scalability is another essential characteristic. As organizations expand across borders or grow in size, their inclusion strategies must be able to scale without losing effectiveness. This requires the ability to customize strategies at different levels of the organization while maintaining a unified approach. For example, multinational corporations may need to implement regional inclusion programmes that reflect the diversity of each geographic area but ensure they align with the overarching corporate values of inclusivity and respect for all employees. This could involve creating regional diversity councils or ERGs that can tailor initiatives to local needs, while still fostering a sense of belonging within the global corporate culture.

Additionally, future frameworks must be **responsive to political polarization**. In many regions, particularly in politically charged environments, issues related to inclusion and diversity have become deeply polarized. For instance, some communities or political groups may perceive inclusion initiatives as threats to traditional values or as political tools, which can result in resistance, backlash, or even legal challenges. A future inclusion framework should be designed with flexibility to engage in constructive dialogue with diverse stakeholders, acknowledge political sensitivities and find common ground where possible. This could include offering open forums, educational resources and strategic partnerships with community groups to foster understanding and bridge divides.

Data-driven decision-making is also critical in shaping future inclusion frameworks. Organizations will need robust systems for tracking and analyzing data on workforce demographics, employee satisfaction and the effectiveness of inclusion programmes. Data helps inform policy changes, measure progress towards goals and identify gaps in current strategies. However, future inclusion frameworks must prioritize **privacy, ethics and transparency** when handling data, particularly when it comes to sensitive topics such as race, gender and disability. Ensuring that data collection methods are ethical and that the information is used to drive positive change, without reinforcing harmful stereotypes or biases, is vital for building trust among employees and stakeholders.

Moreover, **continuous learning** will be crucial for organizations to adapt to evolving trends and social expectations around diversity and inclusion. This includes training leaders and employees on emerging issues such as intersectionality, unconscious bias and evolving legal frameworks. By fostering a culture of ongoing education and reflection, organizations can remain agile and responsive in their approach to inclusion.

Lastly, **employee voice and community engagement** will be at the heart of future inclusion frameworks. Organizations will need to involve their employees at all levels in the development and execution of inclusion strategies. Listening to diverse perspectives – whether through surveys, focus groups, or employee-led resource groups – helps organizations understand the lived experiences of their workforce and identify areas for improvement. Engaging with local communities, activists and thought leaders can also ensure that inclusion initiatives reflect broader societal movements and foster connections that transcend organizational boundaries.

In conclusion, future inclusion engagement frameworks must be dynamic and multifaceted, recognizing that the global and political landscape is constantly shifting. These frameworks should be adaptable, culturally sensitive, scalable and data-driven, while also embracing continuous learning and prioritizing employee engagement. By creating strategies that are context-aware and responsive to local and global changes, organizations will be better positioned to promote a truly inclusive environment that reflects the needs and values of an increasingly diverse world.

1. 'When in Rome,' 'Embassy,' and 'Advocate'

One such framework includes the 'When in Rome', 'Embassy' and 'Advocate' models. These approaches provide structured pathways for navigating complex environments while ensuring inclusion remains a priority. Here's how these models can guide future inclusion efforts. The three models provide a strategic spectrum for companies operating in environments where inclusion principles may be culturally or politically contentious. Originally designed to help multinational corporations support LGBTQ+ inclusion in areas resistant to such initiatives, these models offer a framework adaptable to broader inclusion considerations. Here's a closer look:

'When in Rome' Model

In this approach, organizations align with local norms, laws and practices, even if this alignment requires them to limit or adjust their inclusion initiatives. As many have pointed out, while this model may allow companies to maintain local goodwill and operate smoothly, it can lead to compromised inclusion principles, potentially sending a message of inconsistency. For example, a company may refrain from openly supporting LGBTQ+ employees in a country with anti-LGBTQ+ laws to avoid legal risks or backlash. Critics argue that this model risks alienating employees who expect companies to uphold inclusion values universally and that it could undermine employee trust and loyalty over time.

'Embassy' Model

This model allows companies to foster inclusive practices internally without challenging broader societal norms, effectively creating an 'embassy' for inclusion within their own walls. Corporate strategy expert suggest that this approach can provide a safer environment for marginalized employees while maintaining stability in regions with restrictive policies. For instance, a global corporation might have LGBTQ+ inclusive policies and ERGs within its facilities, yet refrain from engaging in broader advocacy for LGBTQ+ rights within the local community. This model ensures that employees experience inclusivity at work but does not leverage the organization's influence to promote wider societal change.

'Advocate' Model

The 'Advocate' approach is the most proactive and ambitious, wherein companies seek not only to uphold inclusion values internally but to influence external social norms and even policy. This approach has been employed by many companies, which has taken a public stance on issues of LGBTQ+ rights, gender equality and anti-discrimination laws, even in regions where such views are contentious. By advocating for change, companies embody their inclusion principles in a visible, impactful way. However, it requires significant risk tolerance, as engaging in local sociopolitical matters can lead to backlash, operational disruption, or even legal challenges, depending on the jurisdiction.

2. The Cultural Intelligence (CQ) Framework

Another model that can be used is the CQ model framework that emphasizes the importance of adapting to and engaging with cultural diversity. It includes cognitive, motivational and behavioural elements, allowing organizations to tailor their inclusion strategies to the cultural dynamics of each region. The CQ Framework offers a comprehensive approach to navigating diverse cultural environments, focusing on four key components.

CQ is vital for inclusion initiatives because it provides the tools to understand, navigate and adapt to cultural differences. Inclusion strategies benefit from CQ because it helps individuals and organizations develop deeper empathy, refine communication approaches and ensure that diverse groups feel valued and understood. Through CQ, organizations can break down cultural barriers, reduce biases and promote an inclusive environment where all employees feel respected and empowered.

For example, in a multinational organization, employees from different cultural backgrounds may have varying ways of approaching work, communication and decision-making. A leader with high CQ will understand these differences and adapt their leadership style to effectively engage and motivate diverse teams, fostering an environment of inclusion and collaboration.

CQ also allows organizations to assess and refine their inclusion strategies. By evaluating the effectiveness of inclusion efforts through the lens of CQ, companies can identify areas where cultural assumptions and biases may be limiting their progress, allowing them to make adjustments that promote a more inclusive, supportive workplace culture.

In organizations with teams across various countries or regions, CQ helps leaders and employees manage cultural diversity, ensuring that communication remains effective despite differing cultural expectations. Incorporating CQ into training programmes also helps employees understand the cultural dynamics of their colleagues, reducing misunderstandings and fostering better teamwork and collaboration.

Another benefit of CQ is by assessing the cultural fit and understanding diverse cultural needs, companies can build more inclusive recruitment processes and retention strategies that cater to various demographic groups. High also CQ enables better conflict resolution strategies by helping individuals understand the root cultural causes of disagreements, which can be addressed with sensitivity to all perspectives.

The CQ Framework is a powerful tool for fostering an inclusive and equitable organizational culture. By improving motivation, cultural knowledge, strategic thinking and adaptability, individuals and organizations can navigate cultural diversity effectively and inclusively. This not only enhances individual and team performance but also strengthens the broader inclusion efforts within organizations, contributing to a more globally connected, diverse and innovative workforce.

3. Global Leadership and Organizational Behaviour Effectiveness (GLOBE) Framework

The GLOBE Framework is a comprehensive model that examines how cultural values influence leadership styles, behaviours and organizational practices. It offers insights into how leadership and organizational effectiveness vary across different cultural contexts, providing valuable guidance for adapting inclusion initiatives in a global environment.

The framework categorizes cultures along several dimensions, such as power distance, uncertainty avoidance and individualism versus collectivism, helping organizations understand how these factors impact inclusion efforts. For example, in high-power-distance cultures, inclusion efforts may need to focus on hierarchical fairness, while in more egalitarian cultures, inclusivity efforts might prioritize equal opportunities and open dialogue. By leveraging the insights from the GLOBE framework, companies can create tailored strategies that work across different cultural settings.

Using the GLOBE framework, companies can tailor their inclusion strategies by considering cultural preferences, ensuring that their efforts resonate with local values while still aligning with global organizational goals. This model promotes a more culturally sensitive approach to leadership and inclusion, helping organizations navigate diverse environments more effectively.

4. The Stakeholder Engagement Model

The Stakeholder Engagement Model for inclusion focuses on understanding and integrating the diverse needs, concerns and expectations of both internal and external stakeholders into an organization's diversity strategies. By engaging key stakeholders – employees, customers, community leaders and regulators – organizations can better tailor their inclusion initiatives to local realities, ensuring they are culturally and politically sensitive.

A crucial aspect of this model is establishing two-way communication channels. These channels allow organizations to gather feedback, adjust strategies in real time, and address any emerging concerns.

In practice, this could mean involving community leaders in the design of inclusion programmes, conducting regular surveys or focus groups to gauge satisfaction and adjusting inclusion strategies based on stakeholder input. By keeping stakeholders engaged and informed, organizations can ensure their inclusion initiatives are relevant, transparent and aligned with both internal values and external social expectations. This model also helps to foster greater accountability and buy-in, making inclusion efforts more sustainable and impactful over time.

5. The Adaptive Leadership Model

The Adaptive Leadership Model is a dynamic approach that prioritizes flexibility and problem-solving in leadership. In the context of inclusion, it emphasizes that leaders must be responsive to evolving social and political climates, adjusting strategies as external factors change. This model encourages leaders to assess challenges and opportunities, adapt their approaches to diverse contexts and guide their teams through uncertainty. By using this framework, organizations can remain committed to inclusion even when faced with shifting priorities, societal pressures, or political climates, ensuring long-term success and sustainability of inclusion efforts.

This model emphasizes the importance of resilience and innovation. Leaders practicing adaptive leadership must:

1. **Diagnose the System**: Understand the unique challenges and opportunities within the organization or community and assess how they interact with the broader external environment. For example, changes in legislation, government policies, or social movements can all affect inclusion initiatives, so understanding these influences is critical.

2. **Encourage Adaptation**: Encourage teams to experiment and innovate with new approaches to inclusion, allowing the organization to remain agile. For example, if a political shift leads to resistance against inclusion initiatives, an adaptive leader might pivot to new strategies, such as increasing focus on grassroots advocacy or adjusting messaging to better resonate with different stakeholders.

3. **Leadership as a Guide**: Leaders should provide guidance without imposing solutions. Instead, they create a safe environment for employees and teams to discuss challenges, try new methods and reflect on progress. This approach fosters a culture of learning and growth.

4. **Confronting Conflict**: Adaptive leadership also involves embracing and confronting difficult conversations about diversity, equity and inclusion, especially when these conversations may be uncomfortable. By managing conflicts openly and

respectfully, leaders can create an environment where diverse perspectives are heard and valued.

5. **Aligning Action with Purpose**: Finally, an adaptive approach emphasizes aligning actions with the organization's broader mission and inclusion goals. It ensures that, despite changing circumstances, inclusion remains a core priority, and strategies evolve in ways that continue to support the organization's values.

Overall, this model helps organizations stay resilient and responsive, ensuring that inclusion efforts are not only sustained but strengthened in the face of shifting external conditions.

6. The Intersectional Framework

The Intersectional Framework is an approach that recognizes and addresses the interconnectedness of various aspects of identity, such as race, gender, sexual orientation, socio-economic status and more. This framework acknowledges that individuals may face unique challenges based on multiple, overlapping forms of discrimination or privilege. For inclusion efforts, this means strategies should not treat identity categories in isolation but rather understand the compounded impact of these intersecting factors on people's experiences.

For example, a Black woman may face different challenges than a Black man or a white woman, due to the intersection of both race and gender. By applying an intersectional approach, organizations can design inclusion initiatives that are more inclusive and effective in addressing the diverse needs of all employees. This framework ensures that inclusion strategies are comprehensive, responsive to complex societal shifts, and more nuanced, moving beyond a one-size-fits-all approach. It ultimately fosters a deeper understanding of inequality and promotes equity for individuals with multifaceted identities.

Key benefits of using an intersectional framework in inclusion strategies include:

1. **Addressing Overlooked Groups**: It ensures that marginalized groups who may not fit into traditional categories of diversity are included and their specific needs are met.

2. **Avoiding Generalizations:** It prevents organizations from oversimplifying or generalizing the experiences of individuals based on a single aspect of their identity.

3. **Enhanced Inclusivity:** It allows for a more nuanced understanding of exclusion, ensuring that efforts are not just about increasing representation but also about addressing systemic inequalities.

4. **Improving Organizational Outcomes:** Recognizing and addressing multiple layers of inequality can create a more engaged and loyal workforce, as employees feel seen, heard, and valued for who they are in their entirety.

By embracing this approach, organizations can ensure their inclusion efforts are truly inclusive and impactful for all employees, particularly those who experience multiple forms of discrimination.

WHAT THE FUTURE HOLDS FOR INCLUSION

As organizations continue to navigate the complexities of inclusion, it is likely that the backlash may evolve rather than dissipate entirely. However, as societal awareness around issues of inequality and social justice grows, the expectation for companies and institutions to prioritize diversity and inclusion will likely continue to increase.

With the increasing importance of inclusion, expect more organizations to invest in ongoing inclusion training and education. This will involve not just introducing new policies but also shifting mindsets, encouraging empathy, and creating sustainable, long-term cultural changes. These efforts will be instrumental in addressing backlash and creating a culture where inclusivity is the norm rather than the exception.

As inclusion programmes become more ingrained, there will be a stronger push towards data-driven decision-making. Organizations will increasingly measure the effectiveness of their inclusion efforts using qualitative and quantitative data – such as employee satisfaction surveys, representation metrics and retention rates – to ensure that diversity and inclusion are making a meaningful impact.

The focus will likely shift to accountability mechanisms that address disparities in outcomes.

In recent years, backlash against diversity and inclusion initiatives has intensified, particularly in certain political climates where governments have openly criticized or even sought to restrict inclusion-focused policies. This resistance can make it challenging for organizations to maintain momentum in their inclusion efforts, especially when external pressures influence internal priorities. However, navigating DEI backlash requires a thoughtful and nuanced approach.

As societal attitudes towards diversity and inclusion continue to evolve, it's possible that inclusion initiatives will be subject to greater scrutiny, particularly as political and ideological divides persist. Organizations will need to stay agile and adapt their inclusion strategies to changing social contexts, being mindful of the potential for backlash while remaining committed to creating equitable and inclusive environments.

In the future, companies may need to pivot as political and social climates evolve. Inclusion experts, argue that corporate inclusion leadership must remain flexible, rooted in both an understanding of local dynamics and an unwavering commitment to core values. By utilizing this strategic thinking, organizations can choose paths that best align with their goals and stakeholders, whether they operate solely as safe spaces internally or take on active roles in driving societal change.

The future of inclusion will likely focus more on intersectionality, recognizing that individuals belong to multiple identity groups (e.g. race, gender, socioeconomic background) and that the experiences of these individuals cannot be understood by focusing on any one aspect of their identity. Companies will increasingly recognize and address these intersecting identities in their inclusion strategies.

Proponents of diversity and inclusion work face an immense challenge in fostering inclusive workplaces during times of increased political and social resistance. According to researchers, strategies to navigate inclusion in diverse, often hostile environments can vary significantly, and organizations have several strategic models to consider based on their commitment and local context.

As you come to the end of this book, I want to leave you with a simple yet powerful truth: inclusion is not a destination, it's a continuous journey. It requires intentionality, reflection, and the courage to challenge long-standing norms. Creating truly inclusive and equitable organizations isn't just about policies or representation, it's about shifting the way we lead, think, and operate at every level. It's about building environments where every individual, regardless of their background, identity, or lived experience, feels valued, heard, and empowered to thrive.

Inclusion, when practiced authentically, doesn't just transform internal cultures, it shapes the very products and services we bring into the world. When diverse voices are part of the design, development, and decision-making processes, we create offerings that are more innovative, more empathetic, and more relevant to the communities we serve. Inclusive thinking leads to better problem-solving, stronger customer relationships, and more equitable access to opportunity. Quite simply, inclusive organizations don't just perform better, they build better.

We must move beyond performative gestures and start embedding equity into our business models, leadership styles, customer experiences, and daily interactions. This work will stretch us. It will ask us to unlearn, to listen more deeply, and to act with humility. But it will also empower us to lead with authenticity, to unlock new possibilities, and to build workplaces and products that reflect the richness of the world around us.

Whether you're a senior leader, a frontline manager, a product designer, or someone just beginning your inclusion journey, know this: you have a role to play. Inclusion isn't just HR's job or a social responsibility, it's a strategic imperative. The future belongs to organizations that recognize this and act on it with conviction.

So don't wait for the perfect roadmap or the loudest signal to begin. Start where you are. Listen deeply. Act boldly. And above all, lead with purpose. Because when inclusion is at the heart of what we build, internally and externally, we don't just do better business. We create a better world.

Printed and bound by CPI Group (UK) Ltd, Croydon, CR0 4YY
01/12/2025

14781707-0001